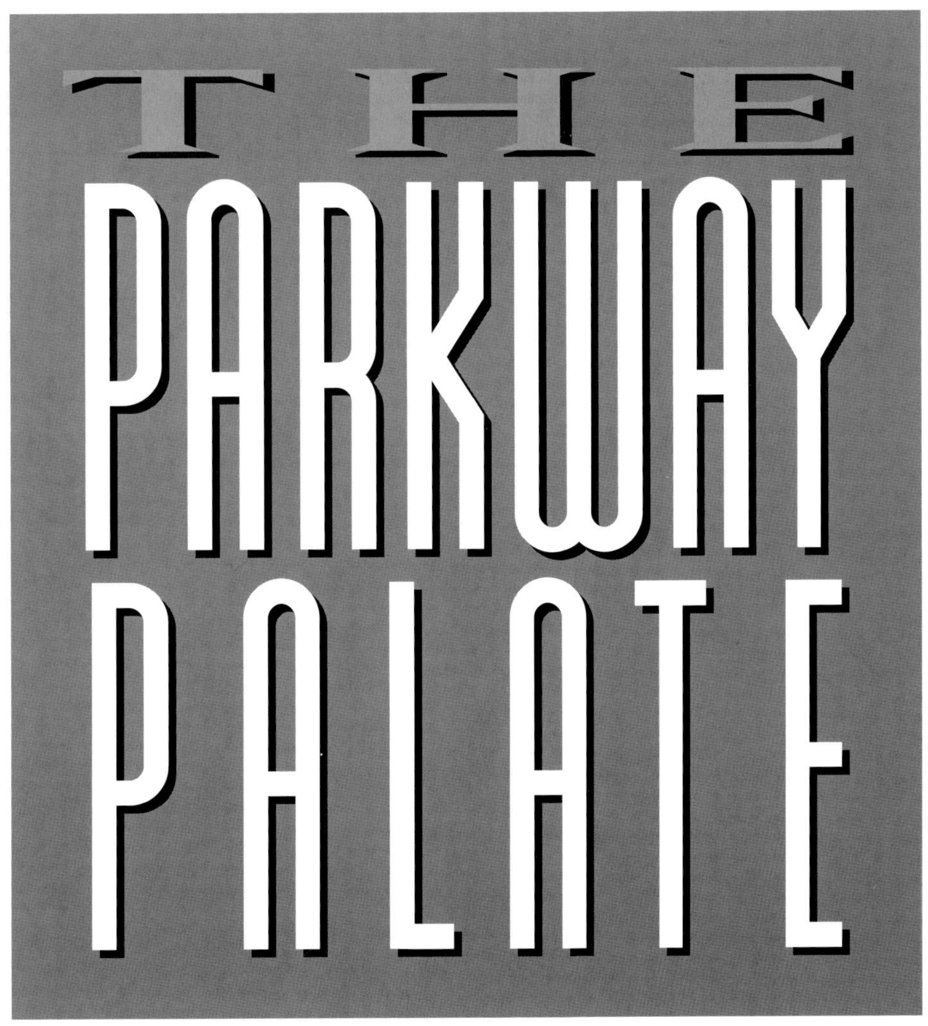

Recipes from the Parties for the Parkway

Edited by Jane C. Groff

Design by Brad Fitzhenry, Vortex Design

The San Joaquin River Parkway and Conservation Trust
1550 East Shaw Avenue, Suite 114
Fresno, California 93710

Printed in the United States of America
First Published in October 1996

ISBN: 0-9654690-0-X
Library of Congress Card Catalog Number: 96-70632

Printed in the United States of America by
Dumont Printing
Fresno, California

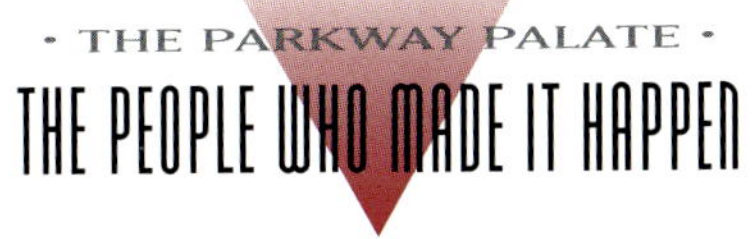

· THE PARKWAY PALATE ·

THE PEOPLE WHO MADE IT HAPPEN

COMMITTEE CHAIRS
Jane C. Groff
Coke Hallowell

HONORARY CHAIRS
Jamie, Thornton & Genevieve Davidson

BOOK & COVER DESIGN
Brad Fitzhenry, Vortex Design

UNDERWRITING PROMOTION
Rick Ataide

COVER STYLIST
Nancy Vajretti

PARKWAY STORIES
Dave Koehler

ADDITIONAL EDITING
Jody Fitzpatrick

EDITING CONSULTANTS
Desa Belyea
Matt Campbell
Gail Marshall
Tim Woods

SECRETARY
Carol Brylka

TREASURER
Terri Figgs

MARKETING/SALES
Jane Campbell

FRONT COVER PHOTOGRAPHY
Scott Shaver

COVER ART DIRECTION
Nancy Vajretti

PARTIES LOGO DESIGN
Paul Zylka

ILLUSTRATIONS
Jean Ray Laury

WRITERS
Linda West
The Fresno Bee Staff Writers

ARTISTIC CONSULTANT
Joyce Aiken

SALES TEAM COORDINATORS
Lynda Daley
Carolyn Nolan

SALES PROMOTION PARTIES
Harland's
Fig Garden Shopping Center

GIFT CERTIFICATE REDEMPTION
San Joaquin River Parkway &
Conservation Trust
Fig Garden Book Store
Valley Lahvosh Baking Company

The Parkway Palate was produced by enthusiastic volunteers, many who are noted professionals in their fields. It is difficult to express the importance of each person who assists in making a project successful—all contribute and all are appreciated.

Volunteers assisted in every step of producing the book; they hosted parties, helped with events, expressed ideas, sold gift certificates in advance to help raise money for printing costs, and have committed to helping with sales after publication. Words alone cannot express our gratitude.

When people of future generations canoe along the San Joaquin River, enjoying the wonders of nature, they should appreciate the efforts made by these people. Our sincerest apologies if we omitted anyone, and a special thanks to future volunteers, unknown at present, who will help market this book.

Robert Ancheta
Marjorie Arnold
Kim Athmann
Larry Balakian
Mary Balakian
Linda Boudreau
Katherine Billingsley
Mike Briggs
Wendy Caglia
Frank Campbell
Jean Chaffee
Sue Clinton
Genevieve Davidson
Diane Davis
Adele Dietl
Milla Drake
Raymond Ensher
Phoebe Farnum
Leslie Fredricks
Helen Giddens
Connie Gough

Joell Hallowell
Margaret Home
Karen Humphrey
Michelle James
Garland Johnson
Stan Kemmer
Carol Kennedy
Cindy Kielmier
Ruby Land
Bev Larios
Lizabeth Laury
Frank Laury
Elaine Lynn
Sue McCline
Peg MacMillan
Barbara Meinert
Debilynn Molineaux
Cheryll Morris
Sabine Morrow
Nancy Niemi

Bob Olson
Cindy Parker
Lucille Pilibos
Heather Porter
Beth Richardson
Skip Rollf
Doris Rose
Sonya Shaver
Sharon Shive
Wendy Shive
David Simko
Melissa Strachan
Stacey Batrich-Smith
Cindy Thorburn
Margaret Thorburn
Janet Van Vleet
Donna Waddel
Anna Wattenbarger
Liliane Wheeler
Jennifer Williamson
Brooke Wissler

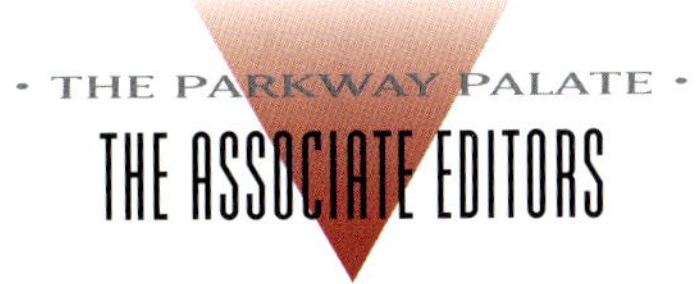

The generosity of the Associate Editors made publication of ***The Parkway Palate*** *possible. They funded the production of promotional materials and events, postage, food testing and a significant portion of the costs to print the first edition of this book.*

We wish to express our heart-felt gratitude to them for giving ***The Parkway Palate*** *such a great beginning.*

RICK ATAIDE, ABBEY PARTY

ELIZABETH B. BONNER

DUMONT PRINTING

PRICE GIFFEN

COKE AND JAMES HALLOWELL

ELEANOR AND HAROLD LARSEN

BETTY LOU AND CLAUDE LAVAL

RAE AND JOHN ROSETTA

MARY AND RUDY SAVALA

SERIOUS READERS ASSOCIATION

SUN-MAID GROWERS OF CALIFORNIA

MARGARET AND JACK THORBURN

ROBERT J. WEIL, PUBLISHER, THE FRESNO BEE

MARGARET WHITTEN

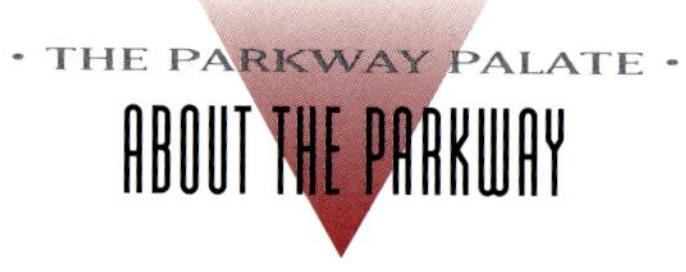

THE SAN JOAQUIN RIVER PARKWAY

More than food comes out of a kitchen. Some of the best ideas and stories in the world are born amidst the fussing and fanfare when friends throw a party. In 1985, Clary Creager and Peg Smith met at Mary Savala's home for what we might consider the ultimate Party for the Parkway. Indeed, it was there on the river bluff—with muffins and freshly brewed coffee in hand—that conversation became the sown seed for what is now the emerging San Joaquin River Parkway.

Ultimately, the San Joaquin River Parkway will be 22-miles of natural reserves, preserved historic sites, parks and trails protecting a cherished natural treasure along the river below Millerton State Park. At the time of this writing, over 1,600 acres are in public ownership, the first two miles of its shared-use trail is completed and three more miles are nearing completion.

It's not too surprising that we're making good progress. The culture of a community is often shaped by its natural resources. Such is the case with the San Joaquin River and those of us living in the valley it has formed. Together, we stand at the crossroads of major decisions affecting the river and our community in the years ahead—determining the breadth and character of the San Joaquin River Parkway as our area develops. It's exciting to be a part of a caring community that has preserved its river for future generations to enjoy. Through lots and lots of friends, a world of good things can happen.

Dave Koehler

Executive Director

About the San Joaquin River Parkway and Conservation Trust

The San Joaquin River Parkway and Conservation Trust is a non-profit land trust formed in 1988. Our mission is to preserve and restore San Joaquin River lands having ecological, scenic, or historic significance, to educate the public on the need for stewardship, to research issues affecting the river, and to promote educational and recreational uses consistent with the protection of the river's resources.

For additional information, please contact us at:
San Joaquin River Parkway and Conservation Trust
1550 East Shaw Avenue, Suite 114
Fresno, CA 93710
Phone: (209) 248-8480 Toll-free: (888) SJR-PKWY
Fax: (209) 248-8474

FOREWORD

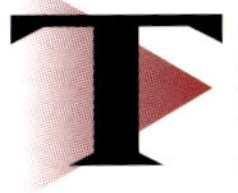

The inspiration for The Parkway Palate arose from Parties for the Parkway events. Parties for the Parkway is an exciting and ambitious fundraising effort, offering over forty parties each year with different themes, menus and entertainment for a wide range of prices. The events are described in a 5 x 6-inch spiral bound booklet published yearly. From cover to cover the booklet is a showcase of inspiration, from party ideas to the original art that illustrates them. Singles join in as comfortably as couples, enjoying canoe rides, picnics, elegant dinner parties with gourmet cuisine, overnight accommodations and limousine rides.

The artists generously donate their work each year for use in the booklet and for later auction; hosts absorb the costs of each party; many musicians and entertainers contribute their talents, letting the dollars generated flow directly to the San Joaquin River Parkway. In the process, these funds are transformed into new trails, restored habitat for wildlife and fascinating programs for young people.

We requested recipes from the hosts, cooks, chefs and caterers who participated in Parties for the Parkway. Many recipes were submitted and most were used. To avoid repetition and provide diversity, a few recipes may differ from the one actually served at the party. A few yearly parties were combined into one. Menus, with wine selections, are provided for some of the parties. The recipes were tested and edited for consistency and accuracy.

The Parkway Palate is a unique book for every taste, containing party descriptions, stories about the San Joaquin River, original art, and some of the best recipes to ever come out of the San Joaquin Valley. Many recipes call for seasonal ingredients. If a special ingredient or spice is indicated, sources are included with the recipe, or a substitute is suggested. You may contact the Parkway Trust Office if you cannot locate an ingredient. We will do our best to assist you.

Parties for the Parkway and The Parkway Palate are proof once again that dedicated volunteers can achieve great things for their community. Their devotion to the Parkway through these projects is deeply appreciated and the results of their efforts will be felt for years to come.

Jane C. Groff　　　　Coke Hallowell

WE DEDICATE THIS BOOK TO THE MEMORY OF OUR FRIEND MADELINE DAVIDSON.

SHE SERVED UP INSPIRATION IN AND OUT OF THE KITCHEN, FEEDING US A SPIRITED DOSE OF FUN AND NOURISHING US WITH HER ENTHUSIASM.

THE ART
THE PARTY
THE PARKWAY

A DAY AT RIVER FAIRE

Hosts: *San Joaquin River Parkway & Conservation Trust*

This premier community event is held each year in May on the banks of the beautiful San Joaquin River. At Lost Lake Park, just below Friant dam, you may stroll with family and friends beneath a canopy of shade trees or canoe the cooling river waters. You might explore an authentic California Indian village, listen to the strains of classical music or join in the line dancing. Try gold panning, an ice sitting contest, a puppet show and a children's run, just to name a few of the attractions which change each year. But one thing you can count on is a plethora of enticing food vendors. Especially inviting is River Cafe, which can be found along a pathway lined with potted greenery. There you'll be seated, pampered and served a gourmet lunch. Try this sampling of recipes of exciting fare from the River Faire!

Artist: Kay Peters Sermon

Firefighters' Chili Beans

There are many food booths at the River Faire. One of the most popular is the barbecue by the Fresno Police Officers' and Fresno Firefighters' Associations. There were several requests for this popular recipe.

Yield: about 1 gallon, plus liquid

1 pound pinto beans
1 teaspoon salt
2 pounds ground round
Salt & pepper to taste
⅓ cup chili powder, or to taste
½ pound bacon, diced
2 cups canned garbanzo beans
2 cups canned kidney beans
2 bell peppers, diced
1 very large onion, red or yellow, diced
2 cups red chili salsa, mild or hot
2 cups brown sugar, or to taste

Use enough water to cover beans by 1-inch, bring to a boil, remove from heat, cover and let beans soak for 1 hour. Simmer beans in water until just tender (2-3 hours), add salt. Season ground round with salt, pepper and chili powder, brown, then drain. In separate pan, fry bacon until crisp (or microwave), drain and cool. Break into bite-sized pieces. Mix all ingredients except brown sugar in a large soup pot, heat just to boiling; add brown sugar, serve.

Jack Coleman, Fresno Firefighter

Tamil Curry

This recipe came from India.

Yield: 8 servings

3 medium onions, chopped
2 tablespoons olive oil
2 cups packaged coconut
1 cup tomato sauce
2 cups stewed tomatoes
1-2 tablespoons curry powder
1 teaspoon salt
Water-enough to make soupy
6-7 boneless pork chops
Sliced bananas, ½ per person
Salted peanuts, ¼ cup per person
Cooked brown rice, about 1 cup per person

Sauté onions in oil until soft, add coconut, tomato sauce, stewed tomatoes, curry, salt and water. Simmer for 1 hour or longer. Add more water as necessary.

Cook pork chops, cut into about 3-inch size pieces and add to mixture. Serve over brown rice. Pass bowls of sliced bananas and peanuts to put on top of the curry.

Jane Campbell

Stuffed Mushrooms

Any leftover filling from these mushrooms is great for stuffing celery.

Yield: 50-80

1-2 pounds mushrooms
2 tablespoons butter
Sherry
1 8-ounce package cream cheese
1 large can (4½-ounces) deviled ham
Parmesan cheese, grated

Sauté mushroom caps in butter until soft, add sherry to taste; drain mushrooms. Mix cream cheese and deviled ham. Stuff mushrooms. Place on large baking sheet, sprinkle with cheese. Place under broiler until lightly browned.

Jane Campbell

AEGEAN ODYSSEY

Hosts: *Pete & Demi Mehas*

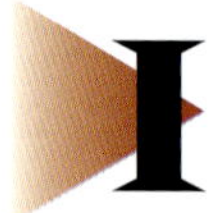

If it's been a while since you visited the Greek Isles, a trip to the bluff-top home of Greek-Americans Pete and Demi Mehas will remind you of what you've been missing. Dinner features succulent lamb as the main entree, of course, with many other enticements prepared and served by Pete, Demi and their daughters. While traditional Greek music plays in the background, guests are regaled with tales of ancient Greek lore. After dessert on the patio, those willing to loosen their ties and kick off their shoes are treated to the excitement of dancing—as the Greeks do it.

Artist: Paul Zylka

Tiropetes

Filo pastry is found in frozen food section of most supermarkets and specialty stores. Also spelled fillo and phyllo.

Yield: about 75 triangles

8 ounces feta cheese
8 ounces dry cottage cheese (strain overnight)
1 teaspoon salt
½ teaspoon pepper
2 eggs, beaten
1 package (1 pound) filo sheets, thaw as directed
½ pound melted unsalted butter

In large bowl, crumble feta cheese and add cottage cheese; mix well. Add salt, pepper and beaten eggs. Blend thoroughly. Cut filo sheets into 4-inch strips lengthwise. Brush a single strip lightly with butter, keeping remaining sheets covered with a slightly damp cloth to keep from drying out. Place 1 tablespoon cheese mixture near end of strip and fold end of filo over the egg mixture at a 45-degree angle. Continue folding flag-style until triangle is finished. Place on buttered cookie sheet. Brush lightly with melted butter and bake for 15-20 minutes at 400°, or until golden brown. May be frozen. Do not brush with butter. Place each cookie sheet in freezer. When tiropetes are frozen, transfer to baggie and seal. To cook, brush with melted butter while still frozen and bake until golden.

Peter & Demi Mehas

Galatobouriko

Yield: 16 pieces

1 quart milk
¼ cup butter
½ cup sugar
½ cup farina or Cream of Wheat
5 eggs
½ cup orange juice
1 teaspoon vanilla
½ cup melted unsalted butter
10 filo pastry sheets, thawed as directed on package

Scald milk, add butter and sugar, heat until dissolved. Gradually stir in farina and bring to a boil. Remove from heat. Beat eggs until light, stir in the farina mixture, orange juice and vanilla. Let custard cool. Custard will still be runny at this stage.

Butter a 9-inch square baking pan and place 1 sheet of filo on the bottom, letting the pastry hang over the sides. Brush with melted butter and cover with 4 more sheets of buttered filo. Pour in the cooled custard, cover with 1 pastry sheet, folding in the edges to fit the top of the pan. Brush with melted butter. Layer 4 more sheets of filo on top, brushing each with butter and folding in the edges that lap over the sides. With a sharp knife, cut through the top layers of filo making 2-inch squares, or on the diagonal into diamond shapes. Bake at 350° for 45 minutes. Custard is moderately set after cooking. It gets firmer as it cools.

Syrup

1½ cups sugar
1 cup water
2 teaspoons grated orange peel
1 cinnamon stick
2 cloves

Mix all ingredients in a sauce pan, simmer for 5 minutes and let cool, strain.

After custard has set, slowly pour cool syrup over pastry. Let cool a few minutes so that syrup will be absorbed. Cut into squares or diamonds and serve warm or cold.

Peter & Demi Mehas

MENU

APPETIZERS

Tiropetes (Cheese-filled triangles)

SOUP

Avgolemono (Egg and Lemon Soup)

SALAD

Greek Village Salad/ Taramosalata (fish roe)

MAIN COURSE

Roasted Leg of Lamb
Pilafi with yogurt
Spanakopita (Spinach and cheese pie)
Stuffed Tomatoes

DESSERT

Galatobouriko (Custard pastry)
Greek Coffee
Fruit

ALL AMERICAN FLOAT

Hosts: *Dave Koehler, San Joaquin River Parkway & Conservation Trust*

Weather permitting, this annual event is traditionally held on the Fourth of July. But one year America's birthday was celebrated in September! Why September, you might ask? Because that year the clouds came, the snow fell and melted, and the water roared fast and mightily down the San Joaquin River. Although the celebration was rescheduled to accommodate capricious Mother Nature, the adventure was worth waiting for. What could be better than a canoe tour of the second largest river system in the great state of California. The trip came complete with a star-bageled breakfast and, after a morning of paddling the waterways, a lunch of barbecued yard bird, presidential potato salad and other delights, was ravaged by the hungry canoeists. Amid old-fashioned hospitality, this was a great opportunity to fly the red, white and blue on this All American Float.

Artist: Robin Gay McCline

Sweet Potato & Snap Pea Salad

Yield: about 10 cups

3 pounds (3 large) sweet potatoes
⅓ pound snap peas, ends snapped off, cleaned
½ large red onion, diced
¼ cup coarsely chopped parsley

Clean sweet potatoes well, but do not peel, cut into ¾-inch dice. Cook in simmering water 5-10 minutes, middle should still be slightly firm as some cooking occurs after removing from heat. Do not overcook. Immediately drain and remove to a flat pan, put in refrigerator to cool. Blanch snap peas in boiling water for 30 seconds, then cool in ice water. While vegetables are cooling, prepare aioli dressing. Toss sweet potatoes with aioli dressing, add peas & onion. Garnish with parsley.

Aioli *(Garlic Mayonnaise)*

3 garlic cloves
3 egg yolks
½ lemon, juice only
¾ cup olive oil
¾ cup canola oil
3 tablespoons water or chicken stock
Salt & pepper to taste

Use a food processor or blender to make aioli. First process garlic, then add egg yolks and lemon juice. Leave processor on and add oils slowly alternating each other. Thin aioli with water or chicken stock to the consistency of mayonnaise. Season with salt and pepper.

Chef Stuart L. Morton, Harvest Grill

Tortilla Bread

A fragrant traditional Native American bread. This bread is a favorite of my family.

Yield: 2 round loaves

2¾ cups all-purpose flour
1 package dry yeast
2 cups warm water
1 tablespoon sugar
2 teaspoons salt
2 cups masa harina or white cornmeal

Mix flour and yeast. Mix water, sugar and salt and add to flour. Stir well, then beat vigorously for 3 minutes. Stir in cornmeal and enough flour to make a stiff dough. Knead 3 to 5 minutes on floured board. Form into a ball, let rise in covered greased bowl for one hour. Punch down, let rest 10 minutes.

Shape dough into two round loaves, and put into two greased round pans or on a cookie sheet. Let rise 30 to 45 minutes. Bake at 375° for 30 minutes. Remove from pans and cool.

Coke Hallowell

PARKWAY MOMENTS

The belt of trees and lush vegetation found along the river's banks is known as riparian habitat. Only two to four percent of California's riparian habitat remains from its historical level in the 1900's. Numerous species of animals depend on riparian habitat for food and cover. Sustaining a healthy riparian zone is essential for preserving our wildlife heritage and water quality. Valley oaks, sycamores, cottonwoods, willows, alders and Oregon ash are the dominant species of trees in the San Joaquin River Parkway. The importance of riparian systems combined with their fast disappearance makes the river a very special place to enjoy, explore and care for.

ART & WINE ENTWINED

Hosts: *George & Lavona Blair, Rick Ataide, Steven Croff, Lockwood Winery*

The Blairs opened their home to a group of sixty art enthusiasts for the viewing of their extraordinary contemporary art collection. Guests were encouraged to sample hors d'oeuvres and eclectic wines, then set free to wander the rooms of the house. George Blair gave an illuminating lecture on the history and work of Robert Cremean, a sculptor whose work is housed in the permanent collection of the Fresno Art Museum, and Blair described the pieces in his own private collection that are destined for the Art Museum at a future date. Soon after, the party retired outdoors to a stylish patio where a variety of dances were demonstrated and guests were encouraged to take a turn tripping the light fantastic.

Artist: Enrique López

MENU

HORS D'OEUVRES

Liver Paté
Chicken, Grape and Walnut-filled Mini Pocket Bread
Caviar Mousse
Miniature Tamales
Smoked Salmon with Cream Cheese
Shrimp Salsa
Assorted Dips and Crackers, Fruits and Cheeses
Yalanchi
Deviled eggs

DESSERT & BEVERAGES

Assorted Lockwood Winery Wines
Kahlua Cake
Coffee

Bernie's Shrimp Thing

Good for a large crowd. This recipe has been around for years and is always referred to by this name. No one knows the origin of the recipe.

Yield: about 24 servings

1 tablespoon Knox gelatin
1 10½-ounce can cream of mushroom soup
8 ounces softened cream cheese
¼ cup mayonnaise
1 teaspoon crushed dried dill
1 bunch green onions, tops included, chopped finely
1 cup celery, chopped finely
½ pound fresh cooked shrimp, shelled, deveined, chopped finely

In a large pan, stir gelatin into soup and let stand 3 or 4 minutes. Warm to just below boiling point while stirring. Add rest of ingredients. Mix well and pour into a 6-cup oiled mold. A fish mold works well. Refrigerate 24 hours. Unmold then decorate with garnish as desired.

Leslie Walters

Caviar Mousse

1 package unflavored gelatin
½ cup cold water

Mix 1 package unflavored gelatin mixture with ½ cup cold water, heat slightly and reserve.

Black Caviar

4 ounces (2 small jars) black caviar
1/3 cup juice from 2 fresh lemons

Rinse caviar gently in cheese cloth in a sieve. Pour lemon juice over caviar, drain, refrigerate.

Egg Layer

4 hard-cooked eggs, chopped
½ cup mayonnaise
¼ cup chopped parsley leaves
1 large green onion, chopped fine
Salt & white pepper
Dash of Tabasco

Mix all ingredients, add 1 tablespoon gelatin mixture.

Avocado Layer

2 medium ripe avocados, mashed
1 large shallot, chopped fine
2 tablespoons lemon juice
2 tablespoons mayonnaise
Salt & black pepper
Dash of Tabasco

Mix all ingredients, add 1 teaspoon gelatin mixture.

Sour Cream Layer

2 cups sour cream
¼ cup finely chopped red onion
2 teaspoons fresh lemon juice

Mix all ingredients, add 2 teaspoons gelatin mixture.

Final Assembly

Line bottom of an 8-inch spring-form pan with foil, extending foil a little beyond rim. Layer in the foil-lined pan: egg layer, then avocado layer, then sour cream layer. Refrigerate until set. Gently spread caviar on top of mousse just prior to serving. May be made a day ahead, but do not put the caviar on until day of serving. Remove sides prior to serving.

Sheri Rainwater

BRIDGE, BRIDGE, & MORE BRIDGE

Hosts: *Joyce Aiken, Jean Laury, Jerrie Peters, Margaret Thorburn, Barbara Hicks, Beverly Daniels, Judy Pierrot, Carol Brylka, Alyce Fourchy, Shirley Valett, Bette Noblett*

Parkway bridge parties have been held in a variety of exclusive settings; from club houses to private homes and luxuriant gardens.

One typical bridge morning, ladies clad in sun bonnets were greeted with flavored coffees, fresh fruit and juices by gracious hostesses, then led outdoors to a wisteria-covered arbor where bridge tables for four awaited. Abundant fresh flowers provided delicate aromas and a feast for the eyes. As each group of four finished its contract, players were served crystal flutes of champagne. When all were finished, an elegant luncheon buffet was offered. A table of delightful desserts provided a finale to a day well spent.

On another occasion, bridge was played indoors accompanied by spa cuisine. Elegance presided as usual, but with reduced calories. The drinks were healthful and the food slimming, even including the exquisite dessert.

Artist: Vicki Mathiesen

Tarts

The family recipe for sugar cookies was adapted into a simple, tasty dessert that can be picked up and eaten, so no forks or plates are required. This is a two-layered tart with a hole cut in the top layer.

These are the tarts
That the knave of hearts
Whisked away
On a summer's Day

Yield: about 18 4-inch diameter tarts

2¼ cups all-purpose flour
2 teaspoons baking powder
1½ teaspoons salt
1 cup butter
1 cup sugar
1 egg, beaten
¼ teaspoon lemon extract
¼ teaspoon vanilla
¼ cup milk
Jam or jelly in assorted colors-such as peach, strawberry, blueberry

Sift flour, resift three times with baking powder and salt. Cream butter and sugar; add egg. Mix until light and fluffy. Add flavorings, then alternate addition of dry ingredients and milk, ending with flour. Stir into a ball and chill for one hour.

Roll out dough on a lightly floured board. Use a round or scalloped cookie cutter, cut circles. Reserve one-half of the rounds, cut a second, smaller circle in center (a ¾ or 1-inch screw-off cap works great). Place a round on an ungreased cookie sheet. Brush the outer ¼-inch rim with water. Add 1 teaspoonful of jam to center. Place a round with small hole in center on top, press edges and seal. Remold scraps of dough into a ball, chill and repeat rolling and cutting process. If tarts are chilled before baking they will not spread as much on the cookie sheet. Bake at 375° for 8 to 10 minutes. Remove cookies before they brown.

Jean Ray Laury

Chicken Curry Salad

If serving a large group, give recipe and exact instructions to two or three friends to make. Combine the salads prior to serving. A serving suggestion: serve with a colorful, chilled soup, such as hot pink cucumber soup and dark Russian bread. Serve on white dishes. Great with a good champagne, served in crystal glasses. Lychees are spelled in various ways. They can be found at most Oriental markets and in the specialty section of some stores.

Yield: 20 cups

Dressing

3 cups low fat mayonnaise
1 tablespoon curry powder
2 tablespoons soy sauce
2 tablespoons lemon juice

Salad

1 11-ounce can lychees, chopped (optional)
8 cups (3½ pounds) bite-sized cooked chicken or turkey breast
1 8-ounce can sliced water chestnuts, drained
2 pounds seedless grapes
2 cups sliced celery
2-3 cups toasted whole blanched almonds
1 20-ounce can pineapple chunks, drained
2 bunches romaine or other dark green lettuce

Mix dressing ingredients. Mix all salad ingredients, except lettuce, combine with dressing and chill for several hours. Serve on fresh, crisp, dark green lettuce.

Elaine Lynn

BRIDGE MENU

Coffees
Fresh Fruit Juices
Champagne
Chicken Curry Salad
Fresh Fruits
Almond Cake and Chocolate Cake
Chocolate Torte en Creme
Decorated Cookies
Cream Puffs
Apple and Peach Tortes
Tarts

CHRISTMAS IN JULY

Host: *Jack & Beth (Marney) Emerian, Karen Yrulegui, Peppino's Italian Cuisine, Robert & Jerrie Peters*

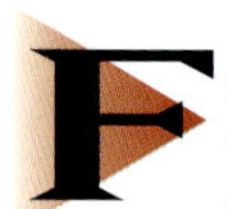

Fresno's historic Christmas Tree Lane provided the backdrop for a progressive dinner party that combined two holidays in one. The evening began with cocktails, hors d'oeuvres and a salad course at the first home. At the next home, the entree was served under a huge canopy in a Japanese-inspired garden where Christmas decorations floated in a nearby pool. Lovely Christmas music was played by a string quartet, red napkins and Christmas candy adorned the green-draped tables, and Santa himself dropped in to issue everyone an early Christmas greeting. As guests strolled to the last home for dessert, they were welcomed at the entrance portal by a holiday wreath of silver stars and American flags. Outside, tables were topped with bright blue covers, center pieces of white daisies, bright confetti and red napkins with white stars. Overhead, twinkling lights reflected in the pool for all those who couldn't wait for Christmas!

Artist: Nancy Winston

Beth's Italian Shrimp Salad

Throw out the iceberg lettuce and use only delightfully delicious lettuces. You must use good olive oil and balsamic vinegar-not the cheap stuff! Make friends with a good Italian Deli. Williams Sonoma, Sam's Italian Deli and Il Forno have the goods in Fresno!

Yield: 8 generous servings

1 cup extra virgin olive oil, divided
1 tablespoon fresh lemon juice
4 cloves garlic chopped fine, divided
Salt & fresh ground black pepper to taste
1 cup white wine: ¼ cup for the shrimp, ¾ cup for the chef
24 large shrimp, peeled, deveined
¼ pound fresh mozzarella cheese, sliced into 8 pieces
2-4 leaves fresh basil, torn. Dried just won't do!
4 tablespoons balsamic vinegar, divided
1 pound assorted fresh greens, washed, dried
1 red onion, thinly sliced
4 plum tomatoes, sliced
2 roasted red peppers, sliced lengthwise

Mix ¼ cup olive oil, 1 tablespoon lemon juice, ½ of garlic, salt and pepper, ¼ cup wine. Add shrimp. Marinate for 1 hour. Sauté shrimp with marinade. Don't cook the heck out of them. Let them cool in their own juice. Set aside.

Marinate mozzarella in fresh basil, salt and pepper, ¼ cup olive oil and 2 tablespoons balsamic vinegar for one hour.

Put 2 tablespoons vinegar, rest of garlic, and salt and pepper in a bowl. Slowly whisk in ½ cup of olive oil. Toss with the greens, onions, tomatoes and peppers. Place on a beautiful low dish with sides. Place shrimp sort of in the middle. Add your marinated mozzarella over the whole thing. Then drizzle a little of the cooled marinade that you cooked the shrimp in over everything. Drink a toast to your culinary talents with the remaining ¾ cup of white wine.

Beth Marney

Fruit Muchen-Apple Pizza Tart

This recipe is from old cooking school days at Paul Mayer Cooking School in San Francisco. Bob Peters and Jamie Davidson (Madeline's husband) took these classes together and Madeline used this recipe a lot, as do we. Our family calls it Apple Pizza.

1½ cups flour
7⅔ tablespoons sugar, divided
¼ pound plus 6 tablespoons butter
4 egg yolks, divided
Pinch of salt
4 tablespoons bread crumbs
2 teaspoons sugar
1¼ teaspoon cinnamon
Sliced fruit of choice (apples, pears, peaches, etc.)
6 tablespoons whipping cream
Red currant jelly or melted & strained apricot jam

Mix flour and 1 tablespoon sugar. Cut in ¼ pound cold butter until mixture is fine as meal. With a fork, stir in 1 egg yolk and pinch of salt. Pat very thin into a 12-inch flan pan with a removable bottom. Combine 4 tablespoons bread crumbs with 2 teaspoons sugar and ½ teaspoon cinnamon. Sprinkle on the dough in the pan. Cover the dough with sliced fruit of choice. Mix 6 tablespoons of sugar and ¾ teaspoon of cinnamon. Sprinkle over fruit.

Melt 6 tablespoons butter, allow to cool slightly, then mix with 3 remaining egg yolks and 6 tablespoons whipping cream. Pour over fruit. Bake 30 minutes in a 400° oven, check for doneness and continue baking another 15-20 minutes, or until the custard and crust are set and browned. Cool 10 minutes before removing the sides of the pan. When cool, glaze the tart with melted red currant jelly or melted and strained apricot jam. Cut into wedges.

Jerrie Peters

HEADING SOUTH

Hosts: *Ron & Julie Miller, Cappie Barrett, Frank & Jane Sanders, Jack & Juanita Schlette*

Guests of this progressive dinner party took a journey through Fresno's Sunnyside district which began with western motifs and ended with an ode to the antebellum south. After cocktails with Armenian and American hors d'oeuvres at the first home, guests sallied forth for salad, and then to an elegant entree served at a southern-style mansion. Flowers and candles floated in the swimming pool and soft lights lit the gardens at the final stop for dessert. A cart laden with liqueurs and coffees rolled among the guests, and a lace-draped table displayed an abundance of flower-adorned desserts. Music for dancing enticed the light-footed to make a truly memorable evening.

Artist: Cheryl Sweeney

Yalanchi

Armenian Grape Leaves

Yield: about 60

1 cup short grain rice
1½ cups water
3 large yellow onions, chopped
1 cup olive oil
2 cloves garlic, chopped
½ cup Armenian parsley (flat), chopped
1 8-ounce can tomato sauce
1 teaspoon dill
¼ teaspoon cayenne pepper
½ cup lemon juice, divided
Salt & pepper to taste
75 canned grape leaves
¾ cup water

Boil rice and water until water is dissolved. Cool slightly. While rice is cooling, sauté onions in oil until limp, in a large skillet. Add garlic and parsley. Mix in tomato sauce, dill, cayenne, ¼ cup lemon juice, salt and pepper. Add cooked rice mixture and cool. Line bottom of roaster with grape leaves.

Place grape leaf, shiny side down, stem toward you. Pinch off any protruding stem. Place 1 heaping teaspoon of rice mixture in center of leaf. Fold stem end over the mixture, then fold in each side to center of leaf. Roll away from yourself, forming a small cigar-like roll. Repeat until mixture is finished. Arrange stuffed leaves, seam side down, side by side, in layers in the roaster.

Mix ¼ cup lemon juice with ¾ cup water. Pour over grape leaves. Cover with another layer of leaves. Cover with a heavy plate then roaster lid. Bake at 325° for 1½ hours. Cool overnight and arrange on platter. Serve cold.

Julie Miller

Southern Greens

Baby greens, fresh from the garden are best, but store bought will do. Ask your green grocer to save the greens from turnips—you may even get them free, until they find out how valuable they are! Substitute chard or kale if turnip greens are not available.

Yield: 6-8 servings

1 bunch of turnip greens
1 bunch mustard greens
1 yellow onion, cut in half, then thin slices.
6 slices crisp bacon, crumbled
1-2 hot chile peppers, finely chopped (optional)
Salt & pepper
Wine vinegar (optional)

Clean greens well. You must wash them two or three times at least. Remove and discard the larger stems by pulling the green leaves off. Put greens, onion, bacon and chile peppers into a pot of water to cover, bring to a boil and simmer until tender, about 1 hour. Younger greens will cook much faster. Salt and pepper to taste. Some people like to add a little vinegar to their greens.

Cappie Barrett

Pineapple-Orange Sherbet

Yield: 8 servings

1 cup water
¾ cup sugar
1 cup crushed canned pineapple
2 cups orange juice
Crème De Menthe

Boil water and sugar for 5 minutes. Stir, add pineapple and orange juice, stir again. Freeze, then let thaw slightly. Put into individual cups. Add a drop of Crème De Menthe on top.

Juanita Schlette

ENGLISH HIGH TEA

Host: *Mary Savala*

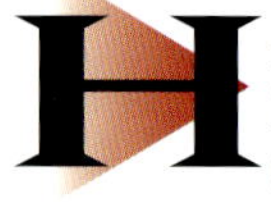

igh Tea is best served on a cold day and always in the most formal room of the establishment. No need for matching tea cups when an assortment of elegant antique cups, each one unique, is always a good way to start conversation. Fresno hostess Cappie Barrett has been known to lend her distinguished collection of china cups for special occasions such as this. Fresh flowers and silver utensils are a must, as are lemon squeezers, a silver tea service and linen napkins. Mary Savala's high tea featured a white-gloved butler, a cook, and maids clad in proper costume. For guests, suits, hats and gloves were the attire and calling cards expected. A pianist in tuxedo lent an ambience apropos to the occasion and Mary's fortunate guests returned home with tea samplers from Fortnum and Mason of London.

Artist: Patricia Hopper

Cream Scones

Make a double batch as guests always want more!

Yield: 1 dozen, about 2-inch diameter

2 cups flour
1 tablespoon baking powder
½ teaspoon salt
2 tablespoons sugar
¼ cup butter
½ cup cream
2 eggs, beaten
Sugar to sprinkle
Flour for pastry board

Sift flour, baking powder, salt and sugar together. Cut butter into dry ingredients. Combine eggs and cream, add to butter-flour mixture. On a lightly floured pastry board, pat dough to ¾-inch thick. Cut into rounds, squares or triangles. Sprinkle with sugar and bake at 375° until lightly brown, about 20 minutes. Serve hot with strawberry jam and lemon curd.

Mary Savala

Tea Sandwiches

Not a meal, just a morsel. Make just before tea. Watercress sandwiches are over-rated. They look pretty, green and white, but have no flavor.

*Stale white bread**
Herbed cream cheese spread
Cucumbers, thinly sliced
Tomatoes, thinly sliced
Butter
Pepper

**Bread that is a little dry will spread better and cut cleanly.*

Cut crusts from the bread, spread with cream cheese and thin slices of cucumber, top with second piece of crustless bread. Second sandwich: spread butter thin on bread, place thin slices of tomato on buttered bread, sprinkle lightly with pepper, top with second bread slice. Cut sandwiches into thirds to finger length, about 1-inch wide. Cover with damp towel until ready to serve.

Mary Savala

Lemon Curd

Yield: 1 ½ cups

3 eggs
1 cup sugar
5 teaspoons melted butter
2 lemons, juice & grated rind

Beat eggs and add sugar gradually, continuing to beat, add butter, lemon juice and rind. Cook in double boiler until thickened, stirring constantly. Cool and store in refrigerator.

Mary Savala

MENU

Tea Sandwiches
Scones with Clotted Cream, Lemon Curd and Strawberry Jam
Fresh Strawberries
Tea Cookies
Petit Fours
Mints
Gateau or Pound Cake
Earl Grey Tea
Lemons

PARKWAY MOMENTS

In 1985, three women found they shared a common goal. Driven by their passionate love for the river and an urgent need to preserve it, Clary Creager, Mary Savala, and Peggy Smith began meeting in their homes with community groups and elected officials. Their efforts rekindled the idea to establish the San Joaquin River Parkway and galvanized the public support needed to begin. Through volunteering countless hours, these and other friends of the river formed the San Joaquin River Committee in 1986 and were instrumental in forming the San Joaquin River Parkway and Conservation Trust in 1988.

HOBNOB WITH HOBGOBLINS

Hosts: *Alex & Elise Moir, Brett & Sarah Hedrick, Jack & Margaret Thorburn, Bill & Barbara Canning, Dawn Jacoby, Joyce Aiken*

Dracula and his evil consort greeted guests with morning coffee and succulent enticements, then spirited them to a waiting coach which whisked them off on a happy Halloween haunt along the fall Blossom Trail. A pirate, deceptively clad as a monk, led the unsuspecting revelers to a children's boat playhouse. Under a briskly flying Jolly Roger, Captain Skeleton steered them to a deserted island on the Kings River where champagne, orange juice and biscotti lessened the sting of capture. Some let the spirits carry them away…on a hayride through the neighborhood! Upon return they joined the others in a devilishly delightful brunch served by spooks, spirits, witches and monks. After the buccaneers buffet, hostages sailed away to a haunted castle for dessert and port wine, and were shortly thereafter released from captivity and transported back to the safety of civilized society.

Artist: Peggy Jelmini

MENU

FALL BRUNCH AT MOIR'S

Fresh Fruit Plate
Dried Blueberry Coffee Cake in Sabayon Sauce
Monterey Eggs
Southwest Breakfast Potatoes with Green Onions, Bell Peppers and Cilantro

DESSERT AT THORBURN'S

Countess Toulouse-Lautrec French Chocolate Cake, Floating in Creme Fraiche with Raspberry Puree Garnish
Margaret's Apple Cake
Coffee, Earl Grey Tea and Award Winning Port

Café Del Rio

Yield: 6 servings

6 demitasse cups
6 teaspoons chocolate syrup
½ tablespoon cinnamon
3 cups double strength brewed coffee
2 tablespoon sugar & cinnamon mixed
1 cup whipped cream

Put 1 teaspoon chocolate syrup in bottom of each demitasse cup, add cinnamon and coffee, stir well. Mix sugar and cinnamon mixture with whipped cream. Put a generous dollop on top of each cup. Serve with a chocolate stir stick.

Elise Moir

Monterey Eggs

Yield: 6-8 servings

1 tablespoon butter
12 eggs, beaten with ½ cup milk
½ pound bacon, cooked, crumbled
½ pound bay shrimp
4 ounces diced green Ortega chiles
1 large avocado, peeled, sliced
Pinch salt & white pepper
8 tomato slices
½ pound sautéed mushrooms
1½ cups grated jack cheese

Coat a 2½-quart quiche pan lightly with butter. Add eggs, top with bacon, shrimp, green chiles, avocado, salt and pepper. Stir lightly. Bake at 350° for 25-30 minutes, until just set. Top with tomato slices, mushrooms and grated jack cheese. Place under broiler until cheese is melted.

A béchamel sauce with bay shrimp or flaked crab meat, or a light cream sauce will complement this dish very nicely.

Bill Hassett, Gourmet Garden Deli, Reedley

Margaret's Apple Cake

Yield: eight 2 x 4-inch pieces

2½ cups firmly packed diced golden delicious apples with skins
1 cup sugar
¼ cup canola oil
½ teaspoon real vanilla
1½ cups all-purpose flour
1 teaspoon baking powder
1 teaspoon baking soda
2 teaspoons cinnamon
2 egg whites
½ cup Sun-Maid® raisins
½ cup coarsely chopped walnuts (optional)

Preheat oven to 350°. Combine apples and sugar in mixing bowl and let stand 10-15 minutes. Blend oil and vanilla with the apples. Combine dry ingredients and mix well. Beat egg whites until fluffy, fold into dry mixture; fold in raisins, apples and walnuts. Pour into greased 8-inch square cake pan. Bake 35-40 minutes. Do not overbake. Cut into 2 x 4-inch squares.

Margaret Thorburn

TOWER RENAISSANCE

Hosts: *Tim Woods & Adams Holland*

Loyal clientele of designers/chefs Tim Woods and Adams Holland were thrilled at the chance to visit the their 1890's home in the historic Tower District. Their interior design work on the turn-of-the-century residence had recently been granted an Award of Merit from Metropolitan Home magazine and was featured in a cover spread in The Fresno Bee's Home Section.

On the day of the party, however, the skies opened up and driving rains threatened no let-up. Undaunted, the convivial hosts ordered a huge white tent that enclosed the entire yard and lent a uniquely festive ambience to the assemblage. The duo's culinary talents resulted in a delightful repast, and provided ample reason why people are talking about the artistic and cooking talents of Tim and Adams!

Artist: Suzanne Sloan Lewis

Baby Lettuce Salad

If possible, buy your salad greens at a farmer's market. The fresher the greens, the better the salad.

Yield: 6 servings

1 pound mixed baby lettuces
Good quality olive oil
Red wine vinegar
Salt to taste
Freshly ground black pepper
1 cucumber, peeled, seeded, diced ¼-inch cut
1 red onion, sliced paper thin
1 shallot, finely chopped

Place rinsed and dried lettuces in mixing bowl, toss with olive oil until just coated. Add a splash of vinegar to taste, followed by salt and pepper. Place equal portions of the greens on six plates, garnish with chopped cucumber, onions and shallots. Serve immediately.

Chef Tim Woods, Echo Restaurant

Wild Mushroom Lasagne

Wild mushrooms are available at farmer's markets; be persistent–it's worth the effort.

Yield: 6 servings

1 pound wild mushrooms washed, cleaned, sliced
1 tablespoon garlic, finely chopped
2 tablespoons butter
¼ cup fruity red wine
Salt to taste
1 pound fresh lasagne noodles
4 ounces grated Parmesan cheese

BÉCHAMEL SAUCE

¼ cup butter, divided
¼ cup flour
2 cups milk

Sauté mushrooms and garlic in two tablespoons butter until mushrooms are limp. Add red wine, cook until most of the wine has evaporated. Salt to taste and reserve. To make béchamel sauce, heat the butter in a saucepan and stir in the flour. Cook, stirring with a wire whisk until thoroughly blended. Scald the milk, strain it into the butter-flour mixture, stirring constantly with the wire whisk until mixture is thickened and smooth.

Cook pasta until limp. Cool in a pan of cold water. In a large, buttered loaf pan, place a layer of pasta, a layer of béchamel, layer of mushrooms and a sprinkling of Parmesan cheese, continue layering until pan is full. Cover and bake in a 350° oven for 1 hour. Let sit for 15 minutes prior to serving.

Chef Tim Woods

Strawberry, Mulberry & Blackberry Shortcakes

Yield: 6 servings

2¾ cups flour
¼ cup sugar
4 teaspoons baking powder
1 teaspoon salt
¼ pound unsalted butter, chilled, cut into small pieces
1 cup heavy cream
1 pint basket strawberries, cleaned, stemmed
1 pint basket each of mulberries & blackberries, picked over & cleaned.
1 cup heavy cream, whipped with ¼ cup sugar
4 tablespoons sugar to sprinkle

Preheat oven to 375°. In a food processor, combine flour, ¼ cup sugar, baking powder and salt with two or three on/off turns. Arrange the butter around the blade and process until combined. With the motor running, pour the cream through the feed tube, stopping just before the dough forms a ball. Turn out the dough onto a lightly floured surface; gently knead, forming a smooth ball. With a rolling pin, roll out the dough to ¾-inch thick rectangle. Using a 3-inch cookie or biscuit cutter, cut out 6 circles, arrange on a baking tray about 2-inches apart. Bake 5 minutes, reduce heat to 350°, bake until the cakes are golden and firm to the touch, 25-30 minutes. Cool on a rack.

Puree strawberries in the food processor. Slice shortcakes in half. Divide strawberry puree into 6 bowls. Place one-half of shortcake on top of puree, fill with blackberries and mulberries; cover with whipped cream; top with remaining halved shortcake. Sprinkle with sugar.

(If no food processor is available, mix flour, sugar, baking powder and salt. Using a pastry blender, cut chilled butter into the flour mixture until it resembles course cornmeal; add cream and gently knead into a ball; turn dough onto a lightly floured surface. With rolling pin, roll out to a ¾-inch thick rectangle. Proceed with recipe instructions above.)

Chef Tim Woods

RETURN OF JOHN MUIR

Hosts: *Dave & Linda Grubbs, Dave & Sharon Koehler*

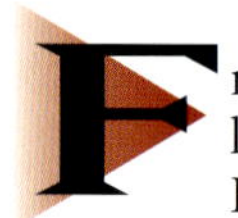

Frank Helling, portraying the great naturalist John Muir, greeted guests with refreshments and led them on a nature walk to a spread on Rank Island, now a part of the San Joaquin River Ecological Reserve. Canoes transported provisions to a bucolic setting on a vibrant green grassy riverbank decorated by nature herself with cottonwood and oak trees. Chef Stuart Morton added his touch with checkered table cloths and napkins set along the banks, each with a four-place setting. Guests enjoyed dinner and home-brewed ale while ice-filled wheelbarrows kept libations chilled. The meal included Muir's favorites, hot tea and stale bread, for those who insisted on authenticity. Ornithologist Dr. Steve Ervin was on hand to explain details of the island's unique heron rookery and, right on cue, a flight of Great Blue Herons glided by.

Artist: Jill Forster

John Muir Mountain Meadow Mist

A hand-made Scotch ale by Jeff and David Grubbs: A commemorative brew to celebrate the preservation of wilderness.

John Muir might have "sauntered", as he put it, down the lovely San Joaquin River seeking refreshment in a libation from his homeland. We made a batch of triple malt Scotch ale for a reception in his honor on Rank Island in May of '94. (History has it that Mr. Muir drank wine but the grape harvest was still months away.)

Scotch ales are a bit malty and only lightly hopped since the hopfields of England are quite some distance away. This was a "wee heavy 90 schilling ale". The strength is even today designated by the original cost of a pint. We made 10 gallons but figured guests would have a courtesy tipple, then switch to wine. Alas, only one bottle of JMMMM survived. It's owned by Frank 'John Muir' Heller, without whom this would have been just another batch of home-brew.

This isn't hard but you'll obviously need better directions than these. There are several good books. The equipment is easy to come by and we'll lend ours to friends of the Parkway.

Pale malt, 16 pounds
Crystal malt, 2 pounds
Toasted malt, one half pound
Hops, 3 ounces English Fuggles & 1 ounce Kent Golding
Yeast, Scottish ale
Priming sugar, 1 cup corn sugar

Mashing

Heat water to 170° while you crack the dry malt in a grinding mill. We did it in two batches. 5 gallons at a time is more than enough to handle. Place the cracked malt in a large cloth bag and the bag in a large container with a spigot or drain. This is the mash tun. Pour hot water over the cracked malt, cover it, and let it stand for 50 minutes. Add more hot water to the mash tun to raise the temperature and let it stand again. Drain the wort (the sugar-rich liquid from the mash tun), sparge (rinse) the mash with even hotter water (180°) adding that to the wort. The left-over mash is a terrific garden amendment. Great aroma too!

Brewing

Bring the wort to a boil–carefully–lest this be the only batch to ever grace your kitchen. Add the Fuggles for taste and boil for 1½ hours. 5 minutes before the end of the boil, add the Kent Golding hops for aroma. Filter the wort through cheesecloth and cool it to room temperature. Add the yeast and ferment the brew for 10 to 14 days in a large carboy.

Krausening:

The main fermentation is over but the carbonation has been lost. Our brew is carbonated by causing a secondary fermentation. Draw the liquid out of the fermentation tank into another container (we use the mash tun again) leaving as much of the yeast sediment behind as you can. Stir in the priming sugar and bottle it in clean, non-screw cap beer bottles. The screw cap ones will break. (You have to buy good beer and empty the bottles to get started with this hobby. That's part of the fun.)

Ferment another two weeks. The beer will keep, even improve over the next couple of months.

PARKWAY MOMENTS

It's been said that rivers are life itself. The combination of water and the constant renewal cycle of a river system creates the most biologically diverse environment we have in the Valley. As a river meanders, eroding soil from one bank and depositing it on the other, it gives life to newly deposited seeds from willows, cottonwoods, and alders while sustaining the majestic Valley oaks and sycamores. The great combination of soils, plants, and river's actions of erosion and deposition creates slightly different plant communities of riparian forest. These communities are related to each other successional, one evolving into the other over time, moving with the river.

LADIES WHO DO LUNCH

Hosts: *Mary LaFollette, Anita Shanahan, Karen Yrulegui, Stacey Batrich-Smith, Coke Hallowell, Anna Wattenbarger, Joyce Aiken*

On the last glorious day of spring, a group of ladies slipped on their finest hats and frocks to attend a seven-course epicurean delight served by seven lovely gourmettes at The Fresno Art Museum. Included in the afternoon frolic was an all-male swim suit fashion show orchestrated by Fresno fashion authority Larry Balakian. Men of all ages strutted their stuff in a variety of swim wear representing years past, present and future. Lunch began with a typical Balakian touch: the first course offered fast food fries, chicken nuggets and onion rings still in their take-out containers. Enjoying a good joke, some dug in with relish, not realizing the real meal was yet to come. Entertainment featured a delightful comedy sketch by Ed Dunn III, portraying "Chef Edward".

Artist: Jean Ray Laury

Mary's Chicken Salad

Yield: 6 servings

3 boneless, skinless, split chicken breasts
1 cup chopped celery
1 green onion, chopped
1 cup fresh or 6-ounce can drained pineapple chunks
⅓ cup sour cream or yogurt
⅓ cup low calorie mayonnaise
1 tablespoon prepared Dijon mustard
Salt & pepper
Assorted salad greens
Fresh basil
Vinegar & oil dressing (any good quality dressing)
½ cantaloupe, peeled & sliced ⅛-inch
1 bunch seedless grapes (Thompson or Red Flame)
Cherry tomatoes
¼ cup chopped or slivered nuts, lightly toasted

Bake or boil chicken breasts, dice into 1-inch pieces. Toss chicken, celery, green onions, pineapple together. Mix sour cream or yogurt, mayonnaise and Dijon mustard. Blend salad and dressing together. Add salt and pepper to taste.

Mix greens and fresh basil. Toss with a little vinegar and oil dressing; place greens on a serving plate. Put a large scoop of chicken salad on lettuce. Garnish with 1 slice cantaloupe, a few grapes, and cherry tomatoes. Sprinkle toasted nuts on top.

Mary LaFollette

Fresh Corn & Tomato Soup

A thick, creamy, coral-colored soup with truly superb flavor. For a tasty variation, roast, peel, seed, and chop 2 red bell peppers. Add to soup as it simmers.

Yield: 4 servings

½ onion, chopped
1 stalk celery, chopped
Dash cayenne pepper
1 clove garlic
1 tablespoon oil
1 tablespoon fresh minced ginger
5 ears corn (4 cups off the cob, frozen corn okay)
4 good-sized tomatoes (canned okay)
½ cup water
½ to 1 teaspoon salt
Handful of fresh cilantro, lightly chopped

Sauté onion, celery, cayenne if desired, and garlic in oil in a heavy 2-quart pan until tender, add ginger. Keep heat low and stir frequently.

Strip corn from cobs with a small, sharp knife. Remove stem end of tomatoes and cut up coarsely. Add corn and tomatoes, water and salt to sautéed vegetables. Bring to a boil; then reduce heat to low and simmer, covered, until corn is tender, about ½ hour. The soup is pretty now, but even better if you take your courage in hand and proceed with the next step. Puree it all. Return to pot, thinning with a little more water if you want, and correct the salt. Heat, sprinkle cilantro on top just at serving time.

Coke Hallowell

PARKWAY MOMENTS

In early spring, the long blue-to-purple flowers of bush lupine decorate the river's banks. A member of the pea family, these blooming plants announce the beginning of canoe season. However, the flowers don't last long and it's only the early canoeists of the year that get to see their beautiful array. In the summer, the lupine's silvery-grey leaves blend in with the surrounding vegetation and the plant is little recognized until it blooms again the following spring.

LAKEFRONT PROGRESSIVE

Hosts: *Thatcher & Dagne Threlkeld, John & Leslie Fredrick, Barry & Pam Kriebel, Betty Bonner*

Guests were delivered by water taxi for cocktails and hors d'oeuvres on the Woodward Lake dock of Thatcher & Dagne Threlkeld, where garden decorations furthered the party's harvest moon theme. At the Fredrick home, soup and salad were savored on tables draped in white and gold which displayed flower-filled crystal vases against the rich dark wood of the home's interior. Then a cross-lake cruise ferried guests to the Kriebels' terrace, where each place setting was adorned with miniature relish-filled pumpkins and lavish Halloween and Thanksgiving decorations invoked the spirit of autumn. Decadent desserts awaited guests both inside and out of the dockside residence of Betty Bonner, and her charming home provided a fitting farewell to a lovely evening.

Artist: Donna Locati

Woodward Lake Clam Dip

This is a favorite recipe from my very first cookbook (Sunset) purchased after my 1955 marriage; a book that is now in tatters.

Yield: 1 pint

1 6-ounce can minced clams
Juice of ½ lemon
8 ounces cream cheese
⅓ cup mayonnaise (more or less)
1 tablespoon chives
4 cloves, crushed, crumbled

Open can of clams, drain and cover with lemon juice. Mix cream cheese, mayonnaise, chives and crushed cloves. Add clams and lemon juice. Mix well. Mixture will be lumpy and slightly stiff. Mayonnaise and lemon juice can be adjusted to get any desired consistency. Serve with strong potato chips. Ruffles or Cape Cod Chips are good.

Dagne Threlkeld

Grand Marnier Strawberry Soup

Yield: 6 servings

3 pints fresh strawberries, sliced, reserve 6 for garnish
1½ cups fresh orange juice (4-5 five oranges)
¼ cup Grand Marnier
3 tablespoons sugar
1 cup crème fraîche

Reserve 6 strawberries. Puree rest of sliced berries in a blender or food processor with rest of ingredients. Pour into a large bowl, cover and chill for one hour. Serve in shallow bowls or large balloon wine glasses. Slice a strawberry on each serving and float an edible flower on each.

Crème Fraîche

Combine 2 tablespoons buttermilk to 1 cup whipping cream in glass container. Cover and let stand at room temperature for 24 hours, or until very thick. Stir well and refrigerate for up to 10 days.

Leslie Frederick

Hazelnut Mousse

Yield: 12 4-ounce servings

½ cup skinned hazelnuts, crushed
1 pound bittersweet chocolate, chopped
2 tablespoons butter, room temperature
1 cup sugar, divided
6 eggs, separated
5 tablespoons Scotch whiskey
Pinch of cream of tartar

Preheat oven to 400°. Spread hazelnuts on baking sheet, bake 10-12 minutes, or until skins crack. Remove from oven; place damp cloth over nuts and let set for a few minutes, then pour nuts into towel; rub nuts in the towel to remove as much skin as possible; put in a zip-lock bag; gently hit with a hammer to crush. Spread crushed nuts on baking sheet and toast until golden brown, about 5-10 minutes. (Note: Nuts burn easily.) Set aside.

Bring a small quantity of water to the simmer in saucepan. Combine chocolate, butter and ½ cup of sugar in bowl. Set bowl over the simmering water. (Note: The bottom of the bowl should not touch the water.) Stir occasionally until the chocolate has melted. Remove bowl from the heat and stir in the egg yolks. Add hazelnuts and whiskey. Stir to combine. Mixture will be very stiff and slightly granular in appearance.

Beat the egg whites with a pinch of cream of tartar until stiff peaks form. Gradually beat in remaining ½ cup sugar and continue beating until stiff peaks form. Whisk approximately ⅓ of the egg whites into the chocolate mixture. With large spatula, gently fold the chocolate mixture into the remaining egg whites.

Pour the mousse into pot de crème pots or individual dessert glasses. Chill until firm, 2-3 hours. The mousse can be made up to 2 days in advance. The flavor will improve as mousse sets.

Travis Ryan Everhart, TRE's Gourmet

HERB FEAST & FESTIVAL

Hosts: *Rosemary Nachtigall, T.D. Friesen, Nancy Vajretti*

uests breathed the fragrance of a purple-blue hillside of blooming lavender as they traveled the road to Squaw Valley Herb Gardens. Designed and run by artists Rosemary Nachtigall and T.D. Friesen, the gardens offer a place to taste unusual fare and to purchase the herb plants used in the special dishes served. Themes change for the ever-popular events held at the gardens. One year guests were encouraged to wear festive dancing garb to help celebrate the earth's changing seasons. Sipping rose petal and orange-mint sangría, they were mesmerized by the drumming and percussion of the West African rhythms of Kalimba-Soundz' and the whale and dolphin acoustic guitar magic of Scott Huckabay. A garden stroll and commentary with Rosemary or a view of the etched stone work of T.D. is always a treat. The hosts may serve up favorite foods from Old Mexico or cajole Nancy Vajretti into providing some of her Italian specialties. You're sure to enjoy your journey to this magical land.

Artist: T.D. Friesen

Rosemary's Saged Frybread

These golden-brown crispy-fried tortillas are delicious on their own, with cinnamon-sugar, or as they are served at the gardens, vegetarian style, with grated cheese, refried beans, Spanish rice, fresh tomato salsa and topped with sour cream. Creative substitutions: Rosemary leaves individually separated or a teaspoon or more of red chilies and/or chopped garlic to add spice.

Yield: 12 servings

2½ cups milk
8 fresh sage leaves (garden or purple)
3 cups self-rising flour
1 cup self-rising flour for the board & patting the tortillas
Canola oil for deep frying

Warm milk to luke warm on low heat in sauce pan. Avoiding the stems, cut sage leaves into thin slices with kitchen scissors and put directly into warming milk. Place flour into bowl, add milk and stir into a soft and smooth batter. You can add more flour to the batter, but if the batter becomes too stiff it will make rock-like frybread, so keep it on the soft side. Shape into small hand-sized balls and let rise.

Heat canola oil to 400°. Flouring hands as necessary, pat each ball into tortilla shape. Gently put into hot oil. Fry each side until golden brown. Lay on paper towels in large bowl to remove excess oil.

Rosemary Nachtigall, Squaw Valley Herb Gardens

Potatoes Tarragon

This simple casserole dish is always a crowd pleaser at our gardens whether dressed up fancy or presented peasant-style. A 8½ x 12 x 2-inch Pyrex dish works well.

Yield: 6-8 servings

6-8 medium potatoes, peeled, sliced thin
1 5-ounce can evaporated milk
½ stick butter
Salt & pepper to taste
Small amount of regular milk or water
2 cups grated mozzarella cheese, divided
¼ cup fresh tarragon-French or Spanish, chopped medium-fine

Butter heat-proof casserole dish, layer potatoes. In sauce pan, add evaporated milk to butter, salt and pepper to taste and thin with a small amount of regular milk or water. When butter is melted, turn off heat. Stir in 1 cup of mozzarella cheese until melted. Pour evenly over potatoes.

Wash, pat dry, stem and chop fresh tarragon. Sprinkle over casserole. Cover with remaining cheese. Cover casserole with aluminum foil, poke holes with fork to release moisture, bake at 350°, until potatoes are fork tender, about 30 minutes. Cool, cut and serve. Garnish with fresh tarragon. Simply delicious!

Rosemary Nachtigal

Freddie Frittata

A Nancy Vajretti recipe, named by Madeline Davidson. Our first 'ink' from columnist, Madeline Davidson, appeared in her Cabbages and Kings column in 1979. I still serve our Frittata as a brunch item. This wonderful Italian egg dish, cut into triangles or squares, makes an excellent hors d'oeuvre.

Yield: about 18 hors d'oeuvres

12 medium eggs, lightly beaten
⅔ cups artichoke hearts, drained, cut into quarters
2-3 cups vegetables of choice, such as spinach or sautéed mushrooms
½ pound of ½-inch cubes of jack, provolone or cheddar cheese
½ cup bread crumbs
¼ cup diced red bell peppers
2 tablespoons grated Romano or Parmesan cheese
Salt & fresh ground pepper to taste

Add the prepared ingredients to the beaten eggs. Fold together until just evenly distributed. Do not over mix. Pour into a 10-inch quiche dish or 9 x 12-inch Pyrex dish that has been sprayed with vegetable spray. Set dish in a larger baking pan with water ½ way up sides. Bake 45 minutes at 375°. Check center of frittata for doneness with clean knife or skewer. Serve cold, room temperature, or reheat in microwave.

Chef Nancy Vajretti, Gorgeous Foods

LLUNCH WITH THE LLAMAS

Hosts: *Stefan & Mary Biskup*

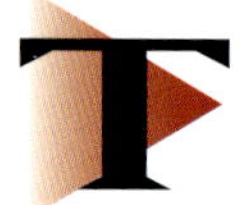

Take a hike with those "Treasures of the Andes"; llamas from the Forked Meadow Ranch near Dinkey Creek. The llamas will carry lunch as you trek the upland meadows to a special picnic site. Checkered tablecloths drape camp tables set up to hold baskets of food and drink, and plenty of time is allowed for guests and llamas alike to graze and enjoy the mountain air. After all and sundry have made their way back to the Biskups' log cabin, guests are invited to relax on the porch, listen to Andean music, and dig into a delicious assortment of desserts and coffees. Each guest is given a llama figurine as a reminder of a remarkable day.

Artist: Carly DeLong

Hikers' Rice Salad

This is a great salad for a picnic that will be transported in a backpack or a llama pack. It has no mayonnaise to spoil or lettuce to wilt, and it's tasty and filling.

Yield: 5-6 servings

1 box Rice-A-Roni fried rice (with almonds)
1 6-ounce jar marinated artichoke hearts, partially drained
2 green onions, chopped
½ bell pepper, diced
1 8-ounce can sliced water chestnuts, drained
1 4-ounce can chopped ripe olives, drained

Prepare Rice-A-Roni as per package directions; cool ½ hour. Cut artichoke hearts into quarters. Add to cooled Rice-A-Roni with ¾ of the artichoke marinade. Add green onion, bell pepper, water chestnuts and olives, mix well. Chill overnight.

Rosie McQuire

Garden Guardian Salad

My favorite tactic for ensuring farms in our future is to support local farmers now. If you buy the ingredients for this salad at a local farmer's market, you will get the freshest, ripest, tastiest food, and encourage local farming to continue in the most direct way possible. My favorite farmer's market in Fresno is The Vineyard on Shaw and Blackstone Avenues. Don't forget your shopping basket!

Yield: 6 cups

1½ cups diced tomatoes
1 large ear fresh sweet corn, kernels only
1 cup sliced Armenian cucumber
¾ cup sliced carrots
¾ cup sweet peppers, your favorite color
¾ cup tender young green beans, chopped
¼ pound alfalfa sprout/sunflower green mixture
½ cup raw almonds, whole or freshly chopped

Combine all ingredients in a large bowl. The fresh ripe vegetables in this simple salad will compliment any summer night and leave your palate refreshed. No dressing is required, but you may choose to lightly dress with vinegar and olive oil.

Mike Biskup

Heat Hammer Smoothie

Children and adults go crazy for this healthy alternative to ice cream. Live apple juice is unpasteurized and very freshly pressed. Odwalla juices are recommended. They are pressed in Dinuba, California, and can be found in many supermarkets.

Yield: 3-4 cups

2 cups fresh strawberries
1 banana, peeled
1½ cups live apple juice

Freeze strawberries and banana overnight (12-15 hours), but no longer, as taste will change. Blend all ingredients in a blender and drink immediately.

Lisa Biskup

Menu

LUNCHEON

Hearty Sandwiches on French Rolls,
choice of Meat or Vegetarian with Cheese
Hikers' Rice Salad
Garden Guardian Salad
Assorted Chips
Baby Carrots and Tomatoes
Roasted Almonds

DESSERTS

Homemade Lemon Meringue Pie
Frosted Chocolate Brownies
Fresh Strawberries
Heat Hammer Smoothie

BEVERAGES

Hansen's Natural Sodas
Cold Bottled Spring Water
Fresh Brewed Vanilla Coffee

MEET THE PRESS

Host: *The Fresno Bee*

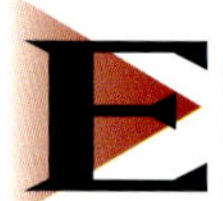

Each year The Fresno Bee offers a unique evening of dining, Q & A, and a special tour of the Bee's production plant. Guests gather at the Bee building and are joined by the publisher, various editors, columnists and other staff members for a get-acquainted reception. Then the ensemble moves on to the staff dining room for a specially prepared feast by a local chef. A tour of the production plant follows, including the state-of-the-art pressroom housing the Flexoman printing press, among the most modern in the United States. Afterwards, the entire group caravans to the Tower District for dessert, a nightcap and celebration of one more edition put to bed.

Artist: Susan Gutiérrez

Summer Vegetable Sauté

Yield: 8 servings

2 tablespoons olive oil
½ tablespoon minced garlic
2 pounds yellow squash, julienne
2 pounds zucchini, julienne
1 medium red onion, julienne
1 medium red bell pepper, julienne
2 sprigs fresh thyme leaves
¼ cup white wine
3 tablespoons fresh lemon juice (1 lemon)
Salt to taste
½ cup Parmesan cheese, grated
½ cup toasted bread crumbs

Sauté garlic in oil to light brown, add vegetables and thyme, sauté a few more seconds, add wine, sauté a little more, add lemon juice and salt if desired. Put in oven-proof casserole dish. Sprinkle cheese on top, then bread crumbs. Bake at 350° for 10 to 15 minutes.

Chef Brad Schwitzer, The Fresno Bee

Green Salad with Mustard Vinaigrette

Yield: 8 servings

1 head romaine lettuce
¼ head chicory
¼ head radicchio
1 daikon radish, medium julienne
4 vine ripe tomatoes, cut in wedges
2 jumbo carrots, julienne
6 basil leaves, julienne
½ cup toasted walnuts
½ cup fresh grated Parmesan cheese

Mustard Vinaigrette

2 cloves garlic, minced
1 shallot minced
¼ cup rice wine vinegar
1 tablespoon Dijon mustard
½ cup olive oil

Wash all the greens, strain, set aside. Prepare radish, tomatoes, carrots, basil; reserve separately.

Place garlic, shallot, vinegar, Dijon mustard in blender or food processor for 1 minute. Add olive oil in a very slow stream. Place greens in a bowl. Mix with dressing. Place on serving plates, garnish with radish, tomatoes, carrots, walnuts and Parmesan.

Chef Brad Schwitzer

Prime Rib

Yield: 8 servings

1 prime rib, bone in
1½ tablespoons kosher salt
3 bay leaves
1 tablespoon oregano
1 tablespoon thyme
2 tablespoons fresh minced garlic
1 onion, sliced thin
Fresh ground pepper to taste

Preheat oven to 400°. Pull up the fat layer of the roast; place all the ingredients underneath and rub them into the roast, then place the fat layer back down. Place in oven and roast 15 minutes per pound, about 2½ hours. Use meat thermometer, remove roast from oven at 135°. It will cook about 5° more as it sits, to medium-rare. After resting, remove the fat, carve roast to desired serving sizes. To make au jus, add 1 cup of water to the pan drippings over low heat. Use spoon to scrape up browned particles until dissolved.

Chef Brad Schwitzer

Horseradish Cream Sauce

Yield: 1¼ cup

1 cup sour cream
¼ cup horseradish sauce
1 tablespoon Tabasco sauce
Salt & pepper to taste

Mix together. Serve with prime rib.

Chef Brad Schwitzer

IN THE NATURE OF THINGS

Hosts: *Hilary Cowger-Kimber, Pam Elam, Steve Jacoby, Harland's Restaurant*

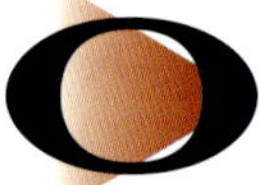

One summer day, landscape architect Steve Jacoby and two of the greenest thumbs on the local horticultural scene, Pam Elam and Hilary Cowger-Kimber, joined forces to lead a tour along the meandering pathways of the beautiful Shin-Zen Gardens of Woodward Park. While enjoying the lovely vista of the gardens from the Tea House, guests took advantage of the opportunity to ask questions and share ideas with the hosts. Anything and everything pertaining to horticulture was discussed. To enhance the scene, terra cotta pots filled with fresh herbs and blue flowers accented blue and white checkered tablecloths. Chef Roy Harland provided a dazzling buffet featuring some of his trademark dishes.

Artist: Marie Bickford

Corn & Goat Cheese Tamales

Make this recipe in early summer when the corn (preferably white) is at its best. Frozen corn may be substituted with decent results, or you can mix half fresh with half frozen. Anaheim chiles can be substituted for the pasilla chiles. This recipe can easily be halved.

Yield: approximately 50 tamales

6 cups milk
20 ears of fresh corn or enough to make 10 cups kernels & scrapings
8 cups masa harina (available in the baking section of most supermarkets)
1 pound butter, melted
2 tablespoons baking powder
1 tablespoon salt, or to taste
2 cups grated jack cheese
2 cups goat cheese (chèvre), crumbled
6 fresh pasilla chiles, fire roasted, stem, seed & charred skin removed, chopped medium dice

In a 6-quart sauce pan, heat the milk over medium heat. Shuck the corn, rinse under cold water to remove all the silk. With a sharp knife, cut the corn from the cob, taking care not to cut too deeply into woody cob. Scrape the cobs well to extract all the sweet juices. Add the corn to the hot milk and bring to a simmer. Cook the corn for 10 minutes, remove from heat. In a food processor, fitted with the steel blade, puree ⅓ of the corn mixture.

In a large mixing bowl, combine the masa, melted butter, baking powder and salt, mix well. Gradually mix in the corn puree, the corn-milk mixture and the cheeses, beating about five minutes with a wire whisk until well combined and fluffy. Fold in the diced pasilla chilies. Refrigerate 20 minutes before rolling the tamales.

Spoon about ½ cup of the tamale mixture onto the centers of 8 x 8-inch pieces of parchment paper, twist ends of parchment to secure. If using corn husks, soak for 10 minutes in warm water. Put mixture in the middle, fold over sides, over-lapping, (or roll into a long cylinder) fold under flat end, tie pointed end with strip of corn husk. Trim tip with scissors, if desired. Steam the tamales, seam side down in a steamer, at least 1-inch above the water level, for 45 minutes. Caution: let steam subside before removing tamales. Hot steam can scald hand and wrist. These tamales may be made ahead and refrigerated up to 3 days before serving. Just heat them in their wrappers and serve with salsa and avocado slices.

Chef Roy Harland

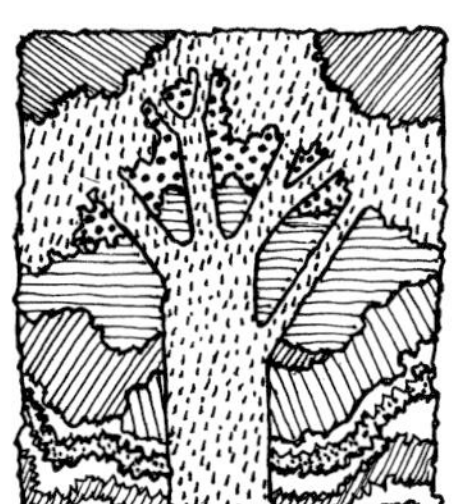

PARKWAY MOMENTS

In 1988, the 286-acre Milburn Unit became the first property to be acquired as part of the Parkway's natural reserve system. Since that time, four additional reserves have been added: the Willow, Rank Island, and Camp Pashayan Units. This San Joaquin River Ecological Reserve now totals over 830 acres and it protects critical habitat necessary to sustain over 250 animal species. The ecological reserve is managed by the California Department of Fish and Game.

NEW YORK, NEW YORK

Host: *Larry Balakian*

o need to travel 3,000 miles to experience the sights, sounds and flavors of New York City. "Partieur" Larry Balakian invited fifty guests to a simulation that began with Manhattans, martinis and hors d'oeuvres served in Fresno's Times Square West. A short stroll to Carnegie Hall West Bistro delivered participants to an eight course 57th Street dinner. Top hats, crowned with a tall candle and surrounded by red apples occupied center stage at tables elegantly dressed with the finest china, silver and crystal. New York maps and brochures graced each place setting, New York posters plastered the walls and dinner was served by waitpersons in appropriate Seventh Avenue attire. The meal was superb, the wine abundant and the entertainment, by Gary Bernstein Unruh and his Carnegie Hall Singers a.k.a. the Community Chorus, was outstanding.

Artist: Michael Mullins

New York Sarma

Yield: About 50

1 cup rice, washed
½ pound ground lamb
½ pound ground beef
2 chopped onions
1 cup minced parsley
1 6-ounce can tomato paste
1 8-ounce can tomato sauce, divided
1 teaspoon mint
1 teaspoon sweet basil
1 chopped ripe tomato
60 grape leaves
3 lemon slices
Salt & pepper to taste
Squeeze lemon juice to taste
Water, as needed

Mix rice, ground lamb, ground beef, chopped onions, minced parsley, tomato paste, 4-ounces tomato sauce, mint, sweet basil and chopped tomato.

If grape leaves are fresh, blanch in boiling water for 3 minutes. Remove leaves, chill in bowl of cold water, drain well. If grape leaves are from a jar, they will be more tender if put in boiling water for about 5 minutes, drain well. Place leaves on work surface with stem toward you, dull side up. Remove stems. Place one heaping teaspoon of the meat mixture on leaf, at the stem end. Roll once, fold in the sides and roll into a neat package. Repeat this process until all the meat mixture is used. Music by Hothouse Flowers is perfect rolling music.

Line the base of a heavy pan with about five leaves and pack the rolls, folded side down, in tight rows. Make as many layers as necessary. Pour 4 ounces of tomato sauce over sarmas, add water to just cover rolls. Top with 3 lemon slices and add squeezed lemon juice. Cover the top with more leaves and an inverted heatproof plate to keep the rolls in place during the cooking time. Bring to a slow simmer, reduce heat. Cover pan and simmer for 50 minutes. Remove pan from heat and allow to cool. Sarma is best served warm and yogurt can be added upon request. Tina Turner's music is appropriate cooking music.

Victoria Balakian

Manhattan Cocktail

Yield: 4 cocktails

8 ounces of bourbon or rye
2 ounces of sweet vermouth
2 dashes Angostura bitters (optional)
4 maraschino cherries, with stems attached

Pour ingredients into a cocktail shaker, filled with ice. Replace cap and shake for 30 seconds. Let set for 30 seconds, then pour through strainer into a shallow cocktail glass. Garnish with a maraschino cherry. If no cocktail shaker available, use a pitcher and stir mixture vigorously with a long handled spoon. Can also be served on the rocks (over ice).

Variations: Perfect Manhattan—use half sweet vermouth and half dry vermouth. Dry Manhattan—use dry vermouth in place of sweet. Rob Roy—replace bourbon with Scotch whiskey.

Larry Balakian

MENU

Ellis Island Hors d'oeuvres

Carnegie Kosher Pickles

Soho Salad

Times Square Souboreg

New York Sarma

Victoria's Shish Kebab

Wall Street Kufta

Broadway Pilaf

Park Avenue Paklava

Armenian Coffee

NORTH VAN NESS TROLLEY

Hosts: *Bill & Anne Lyles, Kevin & Denny Tweed, Emory & Sidney Wishon, Clinton & Deborah Howe, Honda North*

Fellow travelers toasted their journey at the Lyles' home with a glass of sparkling champagne, then it was all aboard the Honda North old-world trolley for a ride to the Tweed's, followed by a visit to the Wishon's, then to the Howe's for a main course prepared by Chef Craig Saladino. Guests enjoyed different architecture and decorating styles and unique art collections at the individual homes along beautiful Van Ness Extension and Van Ness Lake. The end of the line was back at the Lyles' where the evening ended with elaborate desserts and coffee. It was an excursion to satisfy all the senses.

Artist: Joyce B. Aiken

Watercress Soup

Yield: 6-8 servings

2 tablespoons butter
½ onion, peeled, finely chopped
5 potatoes, peeled, thinly sliced
¼ teaspoon tarragon
Pinch of thyme & rosemary
Salt & pepper
5 cups cold chicken stock
6 sprigs watercress, washed, chopped

Heat butter in saucepan. When hot, add onion. Cover and cook 2 minutes over medium heat. Add potatoes and herbs; mix well. Continue cooking, covered, 3 minutes over low heat. Pour in chicken stock, season and stir well. Bring to boil and continue cooking, partly covered, 5 minutes over medium heat. Add watercress to soup; cook 5 minutes.

Denny Tweed

Veal with Mustard Peppercorn Sauce

Yield: 8 servings

8 veal scaloppini
Salt & pepper to taste
¼ cup extra virgin olive oil
1 pound fresh mushrooms, sliced (5-6 cups)
1 tablespoon flour
¼ cup Dijon mustard
1½ cups dry white wine
Green & pink peppercorns to taste

Pound veal scaloppini flat. Season with salt and pepper. Sauté in extra virgin olive oil over medium high heat about 30 to 40 seconds per side. Remove veal, cover and set aside. Sauté mushrooms in the same oil for 3 to 4 minutes. Drain oil and set mushrooms aside.

Make a roux with leftover oil and flour. Slowly add Dijon mustard and wine. Add green and pink peppercorns to taste. Cook to reduce by half.

Add mushrooms to veal and warm for 1 minute. Place veal on plates and spoon sauce over veal.

Craig Saladino

Strawberries Romanoff: The Easy Way

I love to serve this in an elegant crystal bowl, made more glamorous if on a pedestal. Also looks smashing in a silver bowl. The cold dessert creates frost on the silver, making it look more inviting.

Yield: 6-8 servings

1 quart strawberries
¼ cup sugar
½ pint vanilla ice cream
1 cup heavy cream
¼ cup Cointreau liqueur

Wash berries, hull and sprinkle with sugar, chill at least 3 hours. Just prior to serving, soften ice cream slightly. Whip cream until stiff. Beat ice cream until fluffy and fold into cream. Fold in Cointreau and strawberries, reserving a few to put on top. Serve at once.

Anne Lyles

Coffee Tortoni

Yield: 8 ½-cup servings

1 egg white
1 teaspoon instant coffee
Dash salt
2 teaspoons sugar
1 cup whipping cream
¼ cup sugar
1 teaspoon vanilla
1 cup slivered toasted almonds
4-5 coconut macaroons broken into crumbs.
(Save some almonds and macaroons to sprinkle on top.)

Combine egg white, coffee, salt. Beat until stiff, but not dry. Gradually add 2 teaspoons sugar. Beat until stiff and glossy. In a separate bowl, beat whipping cream with ¼ cup sugar and vanilla until stiff. Fold in nuts and macaroons. Mix all ingredients together. Place in individual pot de crème cups or any individual glass containers. They also look great in demitasse cups. Sprinkle with nuts and crumbs. May be frozen in little paper cups.

Anne Lyles

NOUVELLE POLYNESIAN FEAST

Hosts: *Edward & Meroy Nichols*

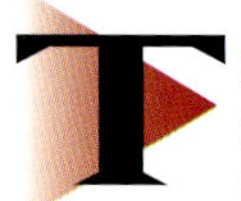

The Nichols' backyard was transformed into a Polynesian paradise for a night of fantastic feasting on succulent delicacies from the Pacific Rim. The evening began with mai tais and pupus, Polynesian hors d'oeuvres, then guests gathered as a roast pig was removed from its spit and carried to a banana leaf-covered table where an apple was placed in its mouth for a formal viewing. A lucky few got to sample the crisp and flavorful pig skin as it was removed prior to carving. Dinner was laid out buffet-style and included Chicken and Long Rice and Lomi Salmon. Lovely ladies in Polynesian dress served dessert and coffee while the Aloha Polynesian Dancers performed under the skillful direction of Vickie Souza.

Artist: Marcia Freedman

Chicken & Long Rice

This is a very popular dish at luaus or Hawaiian poi suppers. The noodle involved in this dish goes by several different names. It is sometimes called rice noodles, cellophane noodles, rice threads, or saifun. Not to worry, they all work just fine and are essentially the same.

Yield: 8 servings

4 ounces long rice-rice noodles
1 small chicken
5-6 cups water
1¾ cup (14-ounce can) chicken broth
8 very thin slices fresh ginger
1 ounce package dried mushrooms, soaked, sliced
1 clove garlic
1 medium onion-sliced
1 tablespoon soy sauce
A few dried shrimp (optional)
Green onions, chopped for garnish

Soak rice noodles in a large bowl of water. This stuff swells! Skin chicken, remove all visible fat. Mix water and chicken broth with ginger, mushrooms, garlic, onion, soy sauce and shrimp. Add chicken, simmer until tender, remove, debone and shred. Remove ginger slices from broth. Drain the noodles and add to stock. Cook until noodles are tender, about 10 minutes. Add chicken pieces. Garnish with chopped green onions. Serve in small, individual bowls.

Edward Nichols

Lomi Salmon

Lomi is the Hawaiian word for massaging, and that is what you will be doing to the salmon. No Hawaiian luau, poi supper or Polynesian feast would be complete without lomi salmon. The popularity of this dish has increased in recent years as a result of more and more exposure to the foods of the Pacific Rim, and it is increasingly being used as a rather esoteric appetizer or salad course.

Yield: 6-10 servings

1 to 1½ salted king salmon
12 firm ripe tomatoes, peel, squeeze out seeds, dice finely
1 medium onion, finely diced
1 bunch green onions, chopped
Crushed ice

Remove skin and soak the salmon in cold water for three to four hours, changing the water frequently. Test for saltiness. Don't cut up the salmon, instead, shred or lomi it into small pieces, discarding the bones. Add tomatoes and onion to the salmon. Garnish with chopped green onions. Cover with layer of crushed ice before serving.

As a serving suggestions, hollow out a large tomato and fill with the lomi salmon. A typical Hawaiian poi supper is served in bowls.

Note: If salted salmon not available, you can make your own by dredging a fillet with rock salt, weighting it down and refrigerating it for a few days.

Edward Nichols

Kahlua Pig

For those who have been to an authentic Hawaiian luau, there is probably a periodic yearning for the succulence of an imu roasted pig. If you do not have access to the right lava rocks, ti leaves, banana stumps and leaves, taro leaves and a backyard fire pit, don't despair. Here is a way to prepare a delicious alternative.

Yield: 8 servings

4-5 pound pork butt
2½ tablespoons rock salt, Hawaiian if available
4-5 tablespoons liquid smoke
Swiss chard leaves, enough to completely wrap the pork

Preheat oven to 500°. Rub rock salt and liquid smoke over pork. Wrap in chard leaves-then wrap with heavy foil-securing well. Bake in a covered pan for 30 minutes. Reduce heat to 325° and cook for 3½ to 4 hours. Shred (do not slice) the meat and serve.

Edward Nichols

ONE FOR THE BIRDS

Hosts: *Kathy Osterberg, Rob Hansen, Stephen Ervin*

The early morning calm along the river begs a walk with nature and a chance to observe and better understand the winged creatures of the San Joaquin. Ornithologist Stephen Ervin and biology/ecology instructor Rob Hansen are on hand to answer questions and enlighten nature lovers on the habits and habitats of valley birds. It could be Rank Island, Willow Unit, or other locations along the river—this is an ever-changing tour as new preserves are acquired and developed. Sharing a picnic breakfast is a good time to exchange fascinating facts about ornithology, Valley history and land use. Whether it's springtime, when more species of birds can be observed than at any other time, or fall, when migration has begun, it's a great time to enjoy a closer look at our feathered friends.

Artist: Donna McCauley

Shrimp & Honeydew Salad with Cayenne-Serrano Vinaigrette

This is a refreshing salad, with subtle tastes to tease your palate.

Yield: 4 servings

Vinaigrette

½ cup peanut oil
2 tablespoons fresh orange juice
2 tablespoons fresh lemon juice
1 teaspoon cayenne pepper
4 serrano chile peppers, stemmed, halved, seeded, thinly sliced
Salt & pepper to taste

Salad

3 bay leaves
3 quarts of beer (water can be substituted)
1 pound large shrimp
1 small honeydew melon, cut in half cross-wise, seed, peel, cut into ⅛-inch slices
⅓ cup finely chopped fresh mint leaves

Put peanut oil in small bowl. Slowly add orange and lemon juices, whisking constantly with wire whisk to form a smooth emulsion. Add the cayenne pepper and serrano chiles, mix well. Season with salt and pepper. Set aside.

Add bay leaves to beer in 5-quart saucepan, bring to a boil; add shrimp and cook 1 to 1½ minutes, just until the shrimp are opaque in the center. Take care not to overcook. Drain shrimp in a colander, cool to room temperature, remove shells and tails from shrimp and devein.

Arrange melon and shrimp plate. Cover and chill. Just prior to serving, drizzle with vinaigrette and garnish with mint. For a picnic lunch, prepare in individual containers. Use small soufflé cups with lids for dressing.

Coke Hallowell

Easy Pumpkin Muffins

Yield: 24 muffins

1 small can pumpkin–for extra moist muffins, use 1 large can
2 eggs
½ liquid required for muffin mix
2 14-ounce boxes of Bran Muffin Mix
1 cup Sun-Maid® raisins
1 cup nuts of your choice, chopped
½ cup sugar & 1 tablespoon cinnamon, mixed

Prepare 2 muffin pans, greased or lined with paper liners. Preheat oven to 400°.

Mix pumpkin and eggs, add liquid in a large bowl, stir well and set aside. Combine muffin mix, raisins and nuts. Add pumpkin mixture to dry mixture, blend until just mixed. Spoon into muffin pans. Sprinkle cinnamon sugar on each muffin. Bake 20 minutes until inserted toothpick comes out clean. Extra moist muffins will retain crumbs on toothpick.

Kathy Osterberg

POWER TO THE PEOPLE

Hosts: *Pacific Gas & Electric Company*

A drive through the beautiful foothills and into the high Sierra by motor coach culminated in an opportunity for a few lucky participants to view the mammoth Helms Hydroelectric Plant at Lake Wishon. Along the way, biologist Garland Johnson provided commentary on the diverse flora and fauna and the complexity of preserving and protecting natural habitats as an integral part of construction projects. At the site, sojourners and their guide descended deep into the mountain toward the heart of the facility–prompting thoughts of immersion in a science fiction movie come to life. Lunch, prepared by the in-house chef, was served in the Helms Plant dining room.

Artist: John Matcham

Pita Pocket Bread

This is a great bread for stuffing with your favorite sandwich filling or left-overs.

Yield: 12

2 package active dry yeast
2⅔ cups luke warm water
2 tablespoons vegetable oil
2 teaspoons sugar
2 teaspoon salt
4½ cups all-purpose flour

Dissolve yeast in warm water in a large bowl. Stir in oil, sugar, salt and 4 cups of flour. Beat until smooth. Mix in enough remaining flour to make dough easy to handle.

Turn dough onto lightly floured surface; knead until smooth and elastic, about 10 minutes. Place in a greased bowl, roll, turning greased side up. Cover with cloth, let rise in warm place (cold oven with light on works) until double, about 1 hour. Dough is ready if indentation remains when poked with fingers.

Punch down dough; divide into 12 equal parts. Shape into balls. Cover and let rise 30 minutes. On floured surface, roll each ball into a 6-inch circle, ⅛-inch thick. Place circles, well separated, on cookie sheets. Cover and let rise for 30 minutes. Heat oven to 450°. Bake until loaves are puffed and golden brown, approximately 10 minutes. Cut into halves. If necessary, use thin bladed knife to open for filling.

Wayne Cadwell, P. G. & E employee

Fruited Chicken Tarragon

This makes a great filling for Pita Pockets.

Yield: 3 cups

Tarragon Mayonnaise

1 extra large egg, room temperature
1 teaspoon fresh lemon juice
1 teaspoons tarragon vinegar
½ teaspoon curry powder
½ teaspoon salt
Freshly ground white pepper, to taste
1 cup vegetable oil

Combine all ingredients except oil in a blender or food processor. With machine running, drizzle in oil. Adjust seasonings to taste. Refrigerate until needed.

Fruited Chicken Salad

2 whole cooked chicken breasts, skinned, deboned, chopped into 1-inch dice
½ stalk celery, cut into fine dice
½ cup Thompson seedless grapes
¼ cup seedless Sun-Maid® golden raisins, chopped
½ bunch chives, snipped
¼ cup nuts of choice-walnuts, pecans, macadamias
Salt & freshly ground black pepper, to taste

Combine chicken with rest of salad ingredients, chill. Add enough tarragon mayonnaise to coat well. Fill pita pockets, or let guests fill. Assorted greens make a nice addition to the sandwich.

Wayne Cadwell

Cinnamon Raisin Bread

(For bread machines)

A cinnamon raisin bread with a little whole-wheat flour and honey to make a wonderfully moist and delicious bread.

Yield: 1 pound loaf

⅔ cup water, warm
2 tablespoons butter or margarine, cut-up
1 large egg, scant ¼ cup
2 tablespoons honey
2 cups bread flour
½ cup whole-wheat flour
1 tablespoon packed light brown sugar
1 tablespoon powdered dry milk
1 teaspoon salt
¾ teaspoon cinnamon
1½ teaspoons Fleischmann's Bread Machine Yeast
⅔ cup Sun-Maid® raisins

Measure carefully, adding ingredients to bread machine pan in the order recommended by the manufacturer. Select sweet or basic/white cycle. Use light or medium crust color. Add raisins at the raisin/nut cycle or 5 minutes before first kneading cycle ends. This is supposed to be a soft and sticky dough. Do not add flour, as the bread will become tough.

Remove baked bread from pan and cool on wire rack.

Sun-Maid Raisins

SOME LIKE IT HOT

Hosts: *Jane C. Groff, Raymond Ensher, Duane & Nancy Niemi*

With the help of flaming torches, African masks, spears and other Ethiopian memorabilia, the tropical backyard of Jane Groff was transformed into an African village. Trays of injera, the crepe-like national bread of Ethiopia, and T'ej, home-made honey wine, were provided at each African print-covered table. African entertainers assisted in demonstrating Ethiopian eating methods and customs such as substituting pieces of injera for eating utensils. Gursha, the centuries-old tradition where the host places the first three bites of food into a guest's mouth, was observed. African beer and T'ej helped soothe the palate after the jolt of spicy-hot Ethiopian food. Guests continued to explore the history and traditions of this fascinating country, assisted in preparation of more injera, and ended the evening with spiced Ethiopian coffee poured into small cups from an authentic Ethiopian clay pitcher. All agreed it had been a truly unique dining experience.

Artist: Sylvia Savala

T'ej

T'ej is an Ethiopian honey wine that can be served with any meal. It is an alcoholic beverage. Traditionally served in birils–small glass bottles with a round body and long neck–but may be served in a wine glass. If left to ferment at room temperature, alcohol content can become quite strong. More honey can be added; do not add more water.

Yield: about 8-12 cups

2-three gallon or larger, deep earthenware or glass containers with lid
2-3 quart cooking pot
Fine-weave cloth bag with tie string, to hold 1½ cups hops
Fine-weave cloth for straining
Masking tape
1 quart honey
1 gallon purified water
1½ cups woody hops (Gesho)

Mix honey with water and put in deep container. Store 3 days in a warm room. Put 6 cups of the honey and water mixture in cooking pot. Put the hops into cloth bag, tie securely and add to pot. Bring to boil, simmer over low heat for 15 minutes. Let cool. Add cooked mixture to remaining honey water mixture and let stand for 5 days.

When mixture ferments, remove hops and cover again for 24 hours. More hops can be added at this time, again in a bag. Taste for sweetness. If too bitter, add 1 cup honey. Do not add more water. Put in air-tight container, seal with masking tape and leave for about 20 days. Filter through fine-weave cloth 7 times. Bottle and refrigerate. Usually after 4-8 days the t'ef becomes strong and sediment collects at the bottom of the container. Pour out slowly. Serve chilled or at room temperature.

Jane C. Groff

T'ibs We't

A fried beef stew. (Note: Careful attention is necessary to prevent burning.) Berbere and jalapeños may be omitted for a mild stew, called A'licha. Berbere-red pepper mixture may be ordered by credit card from C & K Importing in Los Angeles (213) 737-2880.

Yield: 6-8 servings

2 cups chopped red onions
½ cup butter (optional)
1 cup berbere-red pepper mixture
½ cup t'ej or red wine
2 pounds lean beef, cubed.
1-2 jalapeño peppers, coarsely chopped
½ teaspoon cardamom
½ teaspoon fresh minced ginger
¼ teaspoon black cumin
¼ teaspoon fresh minced garlic
¼ teaspoon black pepper
2 cups water
Salt to taste

Cook onions, without grease, in a cast iron skillet, until they turn brownish red color. Add butter and stir. Add berbere and wine, stirring gently. Turn heat to low.

In another cast iron skillet, fry beef, without grease, until tender. Add jalapeños, cook for 2-3 minutes. Add to the cooking onions and stir gently. Add water and keep stirring. Add all the spices and let sauce simmer at a low heat for 15-20 minutes. Serve hot. May be refrigerated and reheated.

Jane C. Groff

Jane's American Injera

Injera is the national bread of Ethiopia. It is used in place of utensils for eating, as a thickener in stews, and as a snack. T'ef flour can be obtained from C & K Importing, in Los Angeles. (213) 737-2880.

Yield: 6-8 Injeras

1 cup self-rising flour
2 cup water, divided
2 teaspoons granulated yeast, divided
1 cup t'ef flour

In a blender, combine self-rising flour with 1 cup water, add 1 teaspoon yeast. Pour into a bowl and let sit for 15 minutes. This portion of recipe can be used to make injeras without t'ef flour.

T'ef flour is difficult to blend with water. You must use fingers to mix properly. Combine t'ef with 1 cup water. When no lumps remain, add 1 teaspoon yeast and let sit for 15 minutes.

Combine both flour mixtures together and mix well. Heat non-stick flat pan on high heat. Ladle or pour about ¼ cup of mixture onto pan, quickly tilt pan in circle to let mixture spread. Cook on one side only until edges just begin to curl. Remove to tea towel for a few minutes to cool, then stack. Best eaten same day, but will last 2-3 days in refrigerator if well wrapped.

Jane C. Groff

SOUTHWEST SOJOURN

Hosts: *Clem & Dorothy Renzi*

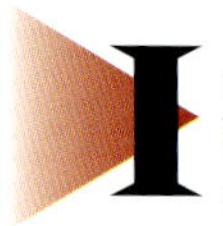

In old Fig Garden, Clem & Dorothy Renzi welcomed guests to their home where furniture had been cleared and replaced with round dining tables draped in shocking pink and sporting centerpieces of cactus and sombreros. Costumed waiters served authentic southwestern cuisine from Fresno's Don Fernando restaurant and poured special label San Joaquin River Parkway and Conservation Trust wine provided by Windsor Wine Company. Professional opera star and voice instructor Dorothy Renzi invited Chef Fernando's four-year-old son to join her at the grand piano where she taught him to play a single note composition. Accompanied by this simple serenade, Dorothy sang to the delight of all assembled. During the evening, guests were able to view and admire many sculptures created by their host, nationally acclaimed artist Clem Renzi.

Artist: Clem Renzi

Gallina Del Puerto

Roasted chicken breast, filled with shrimp and salmon mousse. Served on a Jalapeño-Mango sauce.

Yield: 4 servings

Mousse

1 tablespoon butter
½ medium onion diced very fine
1 pound fresh salmon filet, skinless, boneless
6-8 large shrimp, cleaned, deveined
1 clove fresh garlic
Salt & black pepper to taste
⅓ cup heavy cream

Roasted Chicken

4 8 to 10-ounce chicken breasts, boneless, skinless
4 sheets plastic wrap
4 sheets aluminum foil
1 tablespoon butter or oil
Salt & pepper
4 pieces green chard or spinach leaves
½ cup chicken broth

Place butter in skillet, heat, add diced onion and sauté to golden brown, set aside. Cut raw salmon filet into small pieces. Cut raw shrimp into pieces. Add salmon, shrimp and onion in a food processor with garlic clove, salt and pepper, process until very smooth, then gradually add the heavy cream. Set aside.

Place chicken breast between sheets of plastic wrap. Using a tenderizer hammer, enlarge the breast to ¼-inch thickness. Butter or oil aluminum foil. Transfer chicken to foil. Sprinkle with salt and pepper. Place a green chard or spinach leaf on top of chicken, then spread the mousse, roll the chicken and wrap with foil. Place them in a baking tray. Add chicken broth. Bake at 400° for 30 minutes.

Don Fernando's Restaurant

Jalapeño Mango Sauce

Yield: 5 cups

1 shallot, chopped
2 garlic cloves, chopped
⅓ stick butter
3 tablespoons cornstarch
5 fresh jalapeño peppers, devein, seed, slice
3-4 fresh mangos, peeled, cut into pieces
2½ cups chicken broth
⅓ cup white wine
Salt & black pepper
⅓ cup honey or brown sugar
¼ cup heavy cream

Sauté shallot and garlic in butter until golden, add corn starch, stir 3-4 minutes; add the chopped jalapeños and mango; keep stirring for 3-4 minutes; add chicken broth, wine, salt and pepper to taste, honey or sugar. Let boil for 10 minutes. Remove from heat and pour into a blender. Process until very fine. Pass through a sieve. Add a little heavy cream.

Don Fernando's Restaurant

MENU

STARTERS

Blue Corn Seafood Crepe on a Roasted Red Pepper Sauce
Pineapple-Tomatillo Salsa
Rich Beef Consommé with Mint Albondigas and Vegetables
Pico De Gallo
Chayote, Jicama, Cucumber on Baby Greens with Lime-Chili Vinaigrette

ENTREES

Roasted Pork Tenderloin Filled with Santa Fé Sausage, Corn, Peppers and Fruit, served with Grain Mustard-Marjoram Sauce

Gallina Del Puerto
Roasted Chicken Breast filled with Shrimp and Salmon Mousse on a Jalapeño-Mango sauce.

DESSERT

A Combination of Tequila Mousse and Amaretto Flan

STAR GAZING

Hosts: *Janet Saghatelian, Valley Lahvosh Baking Company*

What better way to celebrate Indian summer than with an evening of divine dining and galactic star gazing from the beautiful Saghatelian home overlooking the San Joaquin River? The evening began with hors d'oeuvres, followed by a mixed grill of meat and fish, and a variety of American and Armenian salads accompanied by Armenian Peda bread and lahvosh. Astronomer Randy Steiner and friend brought two giant telescopes placed on electric tracking to follow the stars as they moved across the sky. They also showed slides taken from space satellites and discussed what astronomers are discovering from photographs of earth taken from space. Back on this planet, guests took delight in spotting a coyote leaping through tall grasses below the deck with a large snake in its mouth.

Artist: Jackie Doumanian

Shish Kebob

This is the original old-country, old-fashioned shish kebob. This recipe is so easy and good, and will save you so much money over buying lamb already marinated. Buy one large leg of lamb, and have the butcher cut it into cubes. Any quality meat market will be glad to do this for you. Shish kebob nestled on a bed of rice pilaf makes a wonderfully delicious meal. To add a marvelous and distinctive flavor to the lamb, use grape stumps instead of charcoal in the barbecue. This gives the meat a delightfully subtle delicious flavor. If Texas can be famous for its mesquite, Fresno should be famous for grape stumps!

Yield: 6-8 servings

1 large leg of lamb, cubed, all fat removed.
¼ cup of extra virgin olive oil.
Salt & pepper
2 large onions, chopped fine
1 bunch flat leafed parsley, chopped fine
¼ cup sherry wine (optional)
2 large onions cut into pieces (approximate width of lamb cube)
2 large bell peppers, cut into pieces (approximate width of lamb cube)
Secret ingredient : a little grenadine juice or pomegranate syrup. This little bit of sweetness enhances the flavor so much.

Place lean cubes of lamb in large bowl, add olive oil and toss to coat. Season to taste with salt and pepper, add finely chopped onions and parsley. Add sherry wine if desired. Tumble together making sure every piece is thoroughly coated. Cover and refrigerate at least overnight; can be marinated for up to one week.

Skewer the lamb, along with large pieces of bell peppers and onions. Barbecue or broil for approximately 5 minutes. Remember, don't overcook your lamb or it will dry out. Stand by and watch it carefully.

If you use long skewers on the barbecue, the best way to remove the lamb is to pull open a wedge of Valley Peda® (not to be confused with pita) bread, wrap it around the meat and pull it off. This was the traditional way, and the Peda used was a highly prized piece of bread. It was always handed to the guest of honor or the host. (Both Valley Peda® & Valley Lahvosh® Armenian breads are made by Valley Lahvosh Baking Co.: 800/480-2704)

Janet Saghatelian

Armenian Salata

This is a wonderful refreshing, tasty summer salad. It was the first salad to disappear at my party.

Yield: 6-8 servings

Salad

2 cucumbers, preferably Goota (Armenian cucumbers)
2 red onions
3 tomatoes, seeded
2 bell peppers, seeded, deveined
Fresh basil
Optional, any of your favorite fresh vegetables

Dressing

1 large clove of garlic, crushed
1 teaspoon Dijon mustard
1 teaspoon Beau Monde seasoning
Juice of 1 lemon
Salt & pepper
¼ cup wine vinegar (select one of good quality)
½ cup light extra virgin olive oil

Select enough vegetables to make a ½ cup serving or more for each guest. Chop all vegetables into bite-size pieces. Whisk together all ingredients for dressing, except olive oil; slowly drizzle in olive oil. Toss dressing with vegetables. This salad refrigerates well and is even better the next day.

Janet Saghatelian

STEEL AND CONCRETE

Hosts: *Jim Lutz, Armen & Dan Bacon, Ed & Terry Grootendorst, David Houck, Richard Branton, Cindy Houck, Ed & Mary Rose Houck*

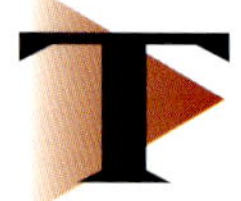

This progressive dinner party took two years to complete! The first one began with an examination of the remarkable style of Fresno architect, Jim Lutz, who escorted guests on a dinner tour of three Lutz-designed homes, including one still under construction. Nancy Vajretti of Gorgeous Foods put her unique talents to use and incorporated building materials and tools as objects of art in her food presentation, which was served amid construction in progress.

One year later the party resumed and many guests returned to view the now-completed home of Dave Houck and Richard Branton. Two other homes were on tour, both conceptualized by the late California designer Vernon Machen, and designed by Jim Lutz. First stop was a contemporary residence, then guests moved on to the essence of Hollywood-Spanish-style, with the hacienda of David and Richard where a guitarist strummed as guests dined beneath an arbor. A short stroll took them to an English Tudor-style home for dessert and continued discussion of design and architecture as combined and beautifully rendered in these three Houck homes.

Artist: Jerrie Peters

Baja Louie

Yield: 6 servings

1 head iceberg lettuce, chopped
1 head romaine lettuce, chopped
3 avocados, peeled & sliced

'Chop Salad' Vinaigrette

3 tablespoons olive oil
½ teaspoon salt
1 teaspoon jalapeños, seeded, deveined, minced
1 teaspoon garlic, minced
1 tablespoon red wine vinegar
1 tablespoon cilantro, chopped

'Chop Salad'

6 green onions, chopped
1 red onion, chopped
4 ripe tomatoes, chopped
3 pasilla peppers, chopped
4 hard-cooked eggs, chopped
Fresh lemon wedges & cilantro sprigs
6 pounds whole crab, fresh cooked, cleaned, cracked

Arrange the lettuce, romaine, and avocado on a large salad platter. Whisk together the olive oil, salt, jalapeño pepper, garlic and red wine vinegar. Toss the onions, tomatoes, pasilla peppers with the dressing. Put a scoop of the 'chop' salad on the bed of greens. Garnish with hard-cooked eggs, lemon wedges and cilantro sprigs. Serve the cracked crab over ice in galvanized buckets. Use several sizes of buckets for garnishes, sauces, silverware, napkins, and more! Serve the Baja Louie dressing on the side.

Baja-Style Louie Dressing

Yield: 5 cups

2 cups chili cocktail sauce
2 cups mayonnaise
1 cup sweet pickle relish
⅓ cup fresh lemon juice
½ yellow onion, grated
½ head celery, grated
6 drops Tabasco sauce

Combine the above ingredients and mix well. Serve with 'Baja' Louie.

Chef Nancy Vajretti

Fresh Corn Tamales

Yield: 2 dozen 4 x 1-inch tamales

3 cups water
3 tablespoons butter
1 teaspoon salt
2 cups fresh corn kernels
1 cup cornmeal
½ cup shredded provolone or jack cheese
1 package corn husks, soaked in water

Heat the water in a sauce pan, add butter, salt and corn, bring to a boil. Slowly add cornmeal, stir, take off heat, add cheese. Let cool.

To make the tamales, form a cornmeal cylinder 4-inches long by 1-inch diameter. Lay corn husk flat, horizontally with pointed end to the right. Place cornmeal cylinder lengthwise in the center, on the left edge of the husk. Fold the upper and lower edges over the cylinder. This will form a tube wrapped in the husk with an open end. With a ¼-inch strip of corn husk, tie a bow at the right side of the tamale, or fold over end. Fold another corn husk in half over the filled part of the tamale and fold the side edges under.

Layer the tamales into a pan with holes or the colander part of a spaghetti pot. If possible stand the tamales on end, tied ends up. Repeat the process until all the tamales have been assembled and layered into your steaming device. Fill the bottom pan or pot with water and steam the tamales for 45 minutes to 1 hour. Caution: let steam subside before removing tamales to prevent steam burn.

To serve the tamales, remove the folded outer husk. Fold back the flaps that have been wrapped around the tube, to expose the tamale in a corn husk "cradle."

Chef Nancy Vajretti of Gorgeous Foods

A TASTE OF PARIS

Hosts: *Sabine Morrow & Maryvonne Gagliarde*

In lieu of flying to Paris for dinner, guests traveled to the Fresno home of French cooking instructor Sabine Morrow for an eight-course dinner of authentic French cuisine. With their own private view of the Eiffel Tower, guests relaxed to the music of Edith Piaf and Charles Aznavour in anticipation of an extraordinary evening of epicurean delights. Fresh flowers graced the elegant table and were found in abundance throughout the house, including one particularly stunning arrangement of long-stemmed flowers. The hosts wore professional chef's coats as they prepared and served a gourmet meal that drew raves from the eager participants. Who needs Paris?

Artist: Benjamin Franklin Locke

Filet Mignon Au Roquefort

Yield: 4 servings

1 tablespoon butter
1 tablespoon olive oil
4 beef filets
Salt & pepper
1 large shallot, finely minced
1 cup port
1 cup beef stock (preferably homemade)
1 tablespoon fresh chives, finely chopped
2 teaspoons Roquefort cheese mixed with 2 teaspoons butter

In a heavy skillet, heat butter and oil until bubbly. Add filets, which have been sprinkled with salt and pepper; cook to desired doneness. Remove meat, set aside, keep warm.

Pour out all but about 1 tablespoon of fat from the pan, add shallot and sauté until soft, taking care to not burn shallots. Add port and reduce until about 1 tablespoon of liquid remains. Add beef stock and reduce by half. Add chives and whisk in Roquefort-butter mixture. Check seasonings, adding a bit more Roquefort if you want a more assertive sauce. Pour sauce over filets and serve immediately.

Chef Sabine Morrow

Potatoes Anna with Basil, Garlic & Red Bell Peppers

Yield: 4 servings

½ stick unsalted butter, divided
1 red bell pepper, clean, slice into ⅛-inch rings
3 large potatoes, peeled & cut into thin rounds, about ⅛ inch thick
4 cloves garlic, crushed
1 teaspoon dried basil or a handful of fresh basil leaves torn into small pieces
Salt & pepper

Preheat oven to 400°. Butter a cast-iron skillet or an 8 or 9-inch cake pan. Sauté bell pepper rings in 1 tablespoon butter until just slightly soft. Set aside. In a small sauce pan, melt remaining butter, add garlic and basil (dried only). Set aside.

Cover the bottom of pan with an overlapping layer of potatoes. Make this first layer neat because it will be the top when served. For the next layer, put about half the pepper rings over potatoes. (If using fresh basil, scatter some over pepper rings, and between each layer.) Drizzle some of the butter mixture over this layer. Repeat the potato and pepper layers until potatoes are used. Remember to drizzle butter between each layer. Salt and pepper last layer.

Bake about 45 minutes, pressing down occasionally with a spatula. When done, run a knife around the pan to loosen, then invert onto a plate. Cut into wedges and serve.

Chef Sabine Morrow

Puff Pastry Bars with Anchovy Butter

Even if you hate anchovies, you'll like this recipe. Trust me! Anchovy butter may be doubled or tripled.

Yield: 18

½ stick unsalted sweet butter, room temperature
2 anchovy fillets
1 teaspoons Dijon mustard
Squeeze of fresh lemon juice (about ¼ lemon)
1 sheet puff pastry, thawed but cold
Egg wash for glaze (beaten egg mixed with a tablespoon of water)

Preheat oven to 425°. Blend first 4 ingredients together to make a paste. Set aside. Cut pastry into bars about 1½-inch wide by 3-inches long (use the seam on the pastry as a 3-inch guide). Brush tops with egg wash. Place cold pastry on ungreased cookie sheet and bake about 20 minutes or until puffed and golden. When done, remove pastry and split each bar sandwich style, spread with anchovy butter and replace top. Serve warm as appetizers.

Chef Sabine Morrow

SUPPER WITH SCHUBERT

Hosts: *James & Coke Hallowell, Joyce Aiken*

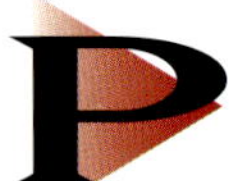

Party-goers wandered the Hallowell's stunning hilltop home and admired their collection of art and artifacts from around the world before a little Schubert was beautifully rendered by The Fresno Musical Club. After the concert, dinner was served outdoors at a long table set beneath the spreading arms of ancient oaks. Colorful napkins, cleverly folded to resemble flower petals, echoed the bouquets of dahlias set among glowing lanterns. Coke Hallowell and Joyce Aiken prepared the 5-course dinner, Parkway waitpersons were on hand to fulfill guests' every whim, and nature did her part by providing a spectacular sunset. As dusk settled, the distant lights of Madera vied for attention with the canopy of twinkling stars. Pianist Fred Savala added a romantic touch as the notes of his piano wafted on the evening air as accompaniment to dessert and champagne.

Artist: Lauren J. Barnes

Chicken Marsala

Yield: 6 servings

3 tablespoons grated Parmesan cheese
3 tablespoons flour, divided
¾ teaspoons salt
Pepper to taste
Pinch of paprika
6 split chicken breasts, deboned, skinned
3 tablespoons butter, divided
½ tablespoons garlic oil
Pinch of cayenne pepper
1 cup mushrooms, sliced
½ teaspoons beef extract, dissolved in water
1 cup water
¼ cup Marsala wine

Combine cheese, 2 tablespoons flour, salt, pepper and paprika. Pound mixture lightly into chicken breasts. Slice chicken into strips. Sauté chicken slices in 2 tablespoons butter for 1 minute each side and remove to a baking dish. Put garlic oil and cayenne pepper in pan and lightly sauté mushrooms, remove.

Melt 1 tablespoon butter in the pan. Stir in 1 tablespoon flour, then the dissolved beef extract. Bring to a simmer, add mushrooms and cook 1 minute. Add wine, then pour sauce over chicken. Bake at 350° for 40 minutes. Serve with baked spaghettini or rice.

Joyce Aiken

Baked Spaghettini

This is an easy and delicious way to serve pasta without the last minute problems that sometimes occur when trying to keep pasta hot, unglued and presentable.

Yield: 6 servings

½ pound spaghettini or other thin spaghetti
1 tablespoon olive oil
1 egg, beaten
¼ cup grated Parmesan cheese
Fresh grated pepper

Cook pasta in salted water and drain. Mix olive oil, egg, cheese and a dash of pepper in a bowl. Stir pasta into egg mixture. Transfer to a buttered pie pan and bake in a 350° oven for 15 to 20 minutes. Cut in pie shaped wedges and serve with Chicken Marsala.

Joyce Aiken

Beef Filet

Yield: 6 servings

1 2-pound beef filet strip
1-2 cloves garlic cut in slivers
2 tablespoons Dijon mustard
2 tablespoons brandy
1 teaspoon salt
¼ teaspoons pepper
4 tablespoons butter
½ cup sherry wine

Cut tiny slits in the meat with a sharp knife and push a sliver of garlic into each cut. Do this on all sides of the filet. Mix mustard, brandy, salt and pepper together and rub onto meat. Let stand at room temperature for 30 minutes. Brown meat in pan on stove top and then roast uncovered in a 400° oven until a meat thermometer registers 135°, medium rare, or cook on a barbecue until medium rare. Remove from roasting pan, cover and let stand for 20 minutes. Melt butter in roasting pan and add sherry wine. Reduce to ⅓ cup and keep warm. Cut meat in thin slices and spoon warm sauce over the meat.

Joyce Aiken

Hot Fresh Peach Sauce

When the summer peaches get ripe this is a refreshing and lovely dessert. It is a recipe that Coke Hallowell gave to me when I lived in the midst of a peach orchard. It soon became my favorite among the dozens of peach recipes I had collected.

Yield: 8 servings

1¼ cup fresh peaches, pureed
3 tablespoons orange juice concentrate
¼ cup sugar
1 tablespoon peach or apricot jam
1½ tablespoons Triple Sec
1½ tablespoons brandy
1 cup sliced fresh peaches

Combine pureed peaches, orange juice, sugar and peach or apricot jam and heat to bubbly. Add Triple Sec, brandy and sliced peaches. Remove from heat. Spoon warm sauce over ice cream.

Joyce Aiken

HAPPY HABITAT

Hosts: *John & Carolyn Nolan, Radanovich Winery*

The Jim Lutz-designed home of John and Carolyn Nolan in eastern Madera County was the site for this food and wine tasting party. Wine was provided by the Radanovich Winery of Mariposa, and a delicious assortment of hors d'oeuvres was dished up by the Nolan family and their friends. Jerry Venturi of Madera House of Music, strolled through the crowd providing foot-tapping accordion music as supporters of the San Joaquin River Parkway took delight in the wildlife habitat the Nolans have nurtured. The Nolan's two-acre property is the home of trophy bass, wood ducks, great blue herons, egrets, red-winged black birds and many other avian species. During the winter migratory season, mallards, cinnamon teal and other ducks make the Nolan pond their stopping place–raising the waterfowl count to nearly 400 birds. It was an appropriate setting for a party to benefit the Parkway!

Artist: Fred Savala

Tasty Tops Mushroom Caps

This simple recipe is quick, easy, and always a hit. Be sure to have plenty.

Fresh mushrooms, small to medium-sized, 3-4 per person
Dried oregano
Jack or mozzarella cheese
Granulated garlic (optional)

Select mushrooms whose caps have not yet opened, to ensure freshness and flavor. Brush mushrooms clean, break off stems, place top down on ungreased shallow baking dish. Stems can be reserved for soup or casserole.

Crush a pinch of dried oregano into each cap. Thickly slice Jack or Mozzarella cheese and cut to just fit inside each cap; press cheese gently into each cap. Sprinkle with granulated garlic, top with additional crushed oregano. Broil until cheese is browned and bubbly. Allow to cool slightly before serving.

Lizabeth Laury of Fresh Fruit & Foods

Tea-Juice Spritzer

A real refresher!

Hibiscus flower tea (raspberry or mint flavors optional)
1 6-ounce can frozen concentrate cranberry-raspberry juice mix
1 liter soda water
Lime or orange slices for garnish

Make a simple strong tea using just Hibiscus flower, or part Hibiscus with raspberry leaf or dried mint. The color will indicate the strength of the mix and steeping time can be adjusted to get just the flavor you desire. I usually make 2 to 4 quarts and mix in a 2 gallon dispenser.

Add 1 can frozen concentrate Cranberry-Raspberry juice mix. Add soda water to dilute for carbonation. Serve over ice with slice of lime or orange.

Lizabeth Laury

Eggplant Steaks

This is one of my favorite foods. Great as a main or side dish.

Eggplant, globe or Japanese type
Tamari-soy sauce
Olive oil
Beer, wine or grapefruit juice
Salt, pepper & garlic (optional)

Select fresh hard eggplant with good color. Slice globe-types into 1-inch thick slabs; slice smaller Japanese-type in half lengthwise. Place in flat-bottomed container and cover with equal parts Tamari (low-salt, high-flavor soy sauce), olive oil and beer, wine, or grapefruit juice; cover all sides. Let stand for 20 minutes to 2 hours, turning to cover all sides. The longer the steaks soak, the tangier they are when cooked. Salt, pepper, garlic or other spices can be added, if desired, but great without them. Grill over coals until browned on both sides on a medium fire. Serve with teriyaki and rice or with a marinara sauce.

Lizabeth Laury

VIETNAMESE STYLE

Host: *Roseanne Guaglianone*

Interior designer Roseanne Guaglianone transformed her home and garden into a Southeast Asian retreat. Guests strolled among Indonesian umbrellas, pots, tapestries and tiki torches, while sipping favorite libations and enjoying Vietnamese music. Colorful Asian prints draped the tables, which displayed fine china and crystal, and sandalwood incense permeated the air. Some of the guests, following Southeast Asian tradition, sat on the floor while feasting on an assortment of exotic Vietnamese dishes prepared by master chef Rudy Liebl. A much needed stretch between courses five and six was master-minded by Kathy Osterberg.

Artist: Shannon Bickford

MENU

FIRST COURSE
Steamed Bitter Melon, stuffed with Pork Paté
Thomas Fogarty wine, 1994 Gewerztraminer

SECOND COURSE
Lemon Grass Soup with Prawns
Vichon wine, 1993 Chevrignon

THIRD COURSE
Warm Duck Salad
Vichon wine, 1993 Chevrignon

FOURTH COURSE
Morning Squash Pork with Jasmine Rice
Chicken Vegetable and Oyster Sauce
Bean Curd Stuffed Tomato
Edna Valley wine, 1993 Chardonnay

FIFTH COURSE
Fillet of Beef with French Fried Potatoes
Benzinger wine, 1993 Merlot

SIXTH COURSE
Watermelon Sorbet
Coffee

Lemon Grass Soup with Prawns

Crab or lobster meat can also be added to the prawns for a variation. Lemon grass adds a subtle lemon flavor. It is available in most Asian markets. Lemon grass grows in large clumps and has long pointed leaves, making a nice addition to any herb or flower garden.

Yield: 10 servings

3 heads of lemon grass
5 cups water
3 tablespoons all-purpose flour
½ cup cold water
1 cup heavy cream
Salt & pepper, to taste
⅓ cup fresh lemon juice
4 tablespoons chopped fresh cilantro
⅓ cup chopped green onions
10 fresh prawns, shelled & deveined

Boil lemon grass in 5 cups of water for 20 minutes, strain, bring back to boil. Mix flour with ½ cup cold water and beat with whisk for about 2 minutes. Add to lemon grass broth. Lower heat and add cream, salt, pepper, and lemon juice. Stir in cilantro and green onions. Add the prawns. Boil for 4 minutes, then serve.

Chef Rudy Liebl, The Ripe Tomato

PARKWAY MOMENTS

Along its banks, the river abounds with long trailing and climbing vines of the California blackberry. Blackberries provide important food and "briar patch" protection for many birds and mammals that call the river home. In writing about the San Joaquin, John Muir observed, "And in midsummer, when the "blackberries" were ripe, the Indians came from the mountains to feast–men, women and babies in long noisy trains, often joined by the farmers of the neighborhood, who gathered this wild fruit with commendable appreciation of its superior flavor, while their home orchards were full of ripe peaches, apricots, nectarines, and figs, and their vineyards were laden with grapes."

WATERCOLOR WORLD

Host: *Patt Rank*

As winter drew to a close, Mother Nature began her annual spring rejuvenation, during which time budding artists captured the beauty of the San Joaquin in their own renderings of a lovely stretch of the river. Well-known watercolorist and instructor Carlene Kostiw led twelve aspiring painters in a private session on Rank Island–one of the Parkway's first additions to the San Joaquin River Ecological Wildlife Reserve Units. Following the class, the artists enjoyed a picnic lunch and compared artistic endeavors. All were able to take home more than just a memory of this special day.

Artist: Carlene Kostiw

Quinoa, Black Bean & Corn Salad

Quinoa is pronounced Keen-wa. It is called "the mother grain" or "the supergrain" as it contains more protein than any other grain, has 8 essential amino acids, and considerably more calcium, phosphorus and iron than does wheat, corn or white rice. It is a small round grain that cooks in half the time of rice and expands to 4 times its volume. It can be purchased in most health food stores, and in some supermarkets and specialty food stores. This recipe is easily halved.

Yield: 14 cups

½ cup fresh lemon juice
1 cup olive oil
½ cup cilantro, chopped
½ teaspoon salt
4 cups fresh corn (8-10 ears)
3-4 cups water
2 cups liquid from poaching corn
2 cups quinoa, rinsed.
1 teaspoon cumin
2 cups black beans, cooked, rinsed
4 tomatoes, seeded, diced
½ cup red onion, minced

Combine lemon juice, olive oil, cilantro and salt to form dressing, set aside. Remove corn from husks, put in water and bring to a boil; remove corn and strain in a colander, reserving liquid. Boil 2 cups of corn poaching liquid, add quinoa and cumin; simmer about 10 minutes or until liquid is absorbed. Cool and add black beans, corn, tomato and onion. Toss with dressing.

Patt Rank

Chocolate Angel Food Cake

Use a 10-inch diameter, 4-inch deep aluminum angel-food tube pan with removable side rim. Adjust rack ⅓ up from the bottom of the oven and preheat to 375°.

Yield: 12-16 servings

1½ cups sifted confectioner's sugar
1 cup less 2 tablespoons sifted cake flour
½ cup less 1 tablespoon unsweetened cocoa powder
1 tablespoon dry powdered (not granular) instant coffee or espresso
1½ cups egg whites, from 10 to 12 eggs, room temperature
½ teaspoon salt
1½ teaspoon cream of tartar, in a fine strainer
1 cup granulated sugar

Sift confectioner's sugar 3 times, set aside. Sift together flour, confectioners sugar, cocoa and coffee, 3 times, set aside. Place egg whites and salt in large mixing bowl. Using electric mixer, beat until foamy. Continue beating while straining in cream of tarter. Continue to beat at high speed until whites hold a firm shape, stiff but not dry. Using a sifter, sprinkle ¼ cup or less of granulated sugar at a time lightly over egg whites, gradually folding in with large rubber spatula. Using the same method, sift flour mixture lightly over the egg whites as you gradually fold them into egg whites. Do not fold or handle mixture more than absolutely necessary.

Pour mixture evenly into the ungreased pan. With a long metal spatula, cut through the mixture in widening circles to cut through any large air bubbles. Smooth the top. Pan will be slightly more than ½ full. Bake for about 40 minutes, until the cake just barely springs back when lightly pressed with a fingertip. Remove and invert pan over a narrow-necked bottle or inverted metal funnel for at least 1 hour to cool.

After cooling, cut around outside edge of cake with sharp thin knife, pressing the blade firmly against the pan, then cut around tube in middle. Gently push bottom of pan to remove the sides. Insert knife between the bottom of cake and the pan and cut around to release the cake. Placed cake plate over the cake, invert and lift off bottom of the pan. Cover with plastic wrap. Let cake stand at room temperature several hours or overnight before serving. Serve with fresh raspberry puree.

Patt Rank

MORE RECIPES MORE PARTIES

Hosts: Rebecca & Gene Gomes, Great Compliments Catering

Mother Nature was the consummate hostess for this party, providing a spectacular sunset for the guests to enjoy from the balcony of the Gomes' river bluffs home. A light evening breeze caressed the diners at the candle-lit repast. The intimate setting was enhanced by soft music playing in the background. Stimulating conversation among new-found friends added all the more to this elegant gourmet dinner party.

Fresh Herb Fromage & Roasted Garlic

Yield: Serves 10 to 12 people

8 ounces Gorgonzola
8 ounces ricotta
8 ounces cottage cheese
½ cup chopped fresh herbs of choice (assorted basils, chives, shallots, rosemary, thyme, garlic)
Large lettuce leaves
2 large bulbs of garlic
Crackers or baguette slices

Fromage

Blend cheeses and herbs together to form into a ball. Place mixture in a cheese cloth bag. Attach top to a dowel or wooden spoon. Suspend over a container to drain. Age in refrigerator for about 3 days. To serve, place in center of a plate of dark greens; place roasted garlic to side of cheese ball. Assorted crackers or baguette slices can be placed around the cheese ball or served separately.

Roasted Garlic

Cut across the heads (pointed end) of garlic bulbs, leaving cloves attached to root end. Marinate in olive oil overnight. Place bulb upside down in baking dish and bake at 300° for approximately 35 minutes. Strain left over olive oil and use for cooking.

Chef Wayne Parker, Great Compliments Catering

Brazilian Steak

Yield: 4 servings

Outside skirt steak, skinned
1 bunch cilantro, finely chopped
¼ cup chopped garlic
¼ cup olive oil
1 tablespoon extra coarse ground pepper
1 cup red wine
1 teaspoons salt
½ teaspoon curry

Roll up steak, cut into quarters and skewer. Combine rest of ingredients and marinate steak at least one full day. Grill over high heat, but do not overcook. The taste will surprise you!

Chef Wayne Parker

Host: Nancy Vajretti of Gorgeous Foods

Guests were greeted with a taste of wine in the tradition of the Italians and invited to pull a stool up to the counter to learn first-hand the secrets behind Nancy's delectable creations. Participation in this class involved all the senses: sight, smell, touch, hearing and best of all, taste.

Turkey Chile Verde

Yield: 1½ quarts

3 pounds turkey, white and dark meat, trimmed & cubed, 1 to 1½-inch
¼ cup olive oil
2 cups chopped onions, white or yellow, divided
8 cloves garlic, chopped, divided
1 teaspoon cumin
1 teaspoon salt, divided
1 teaspoon black pepper
8 tomatillos, husked, rinsed, chopped
1 cup chicken broth
1 teaspoon sugar
2 serrano chilies
2 poblano chilies, or one small can Ortega chilies
1 teaspoon chopped fresh or dried oregano
2 tablespoons fresh cilantro, chopped

Heat olive oil in a large skillet. Add turkey cubes, 1 cup onions, half of chopped garlic, cumin, salt and pepper. Brown turkey cubes. Lower the heat and continue to simmer. In a separate pan, boil tomatillos in chicken broth with the remaining onions, garlic, salt, and sugar. Puree. Add to turkey mixture. Roast the serrano and poblano chiles in a preheated 425° oven until the skins are blistered. Remove, cover with a cloth. When cool enough to handle, peel and seed the peppers, puree, add to the turkey mixture. Add oregano. Taste turkey meat for seasoning and tenderness. If meat is tender and liquids are combined and thickened, add the cilantro. Serve with fresh corn tamale. Enjoy.

Maria Romani, Gorgeous Foods

Pear Salad

Yield: 8 servings

4 fresh pears, any variety
¼ cup fresh lemon juice
1 cup water
¼ cup dried cranberries (craisins)
1 pound assorted baby greens
4 ounces each baby curly endive & radicchio
½ cup choice of cheese (Gorgonzola, Stilton or Roquefort)
½ cup pine nuts, toasted
2 cups sweet croutons (make from nut & raisin bread)
Poaching Liquid Ingredients:
2 cups red or white wine, ½ cup sugar,
1 stick cinnamon, 5 cloves, 2 orange peels

Peel and slice pears in half, lengthwise, leaving stem on one half. Scoop out the core and the tail end of stem that remains in the pear. Put pears in mixed lemon juice and water to prevent them from turning brown. Combine the poaching liquid ingredients in a pot. Simmer for 10 minutes, add pears, cook 12 minutes, test for firmness with a skewer. Pears should be firm. Do not overcook. Add craisins and allow to cool. Clean and drain the greens, arrange on 8 large salad plates. Nestle half a pear in the greens. Sprinkle with cheese, nuts and craisins. Drizzle vinaigrette (see below) over salad and garnish with croutons, serve immediately.

Red Wine Pear Vinaigrette

1 cup olive oil
½ cup red wine vinegar
¼ cup pear poaching liquid
¼ cup raspberry vinegar
¼ cup fresh mint & tarragon
1 teaspoon fresh cracked pink peppercorns

Assemble and whisk all the ingredients together, set aside.

Chef Nancy Vajretti, Gorgeous Foods

Hosts: Pam Elam, Roy Harland

The garden of horticulturist Pam Elam was the setting for an informal dinner alfresco. Sangria and southwestern hors d'oeuvres were enjoyed as gardening enthusiasts toured Pam's garden notable for its herbs, and plethora of flowers including many unusual perennials. A sky of twinkling stars provided a canopy overhead for diners who feasted on a meal featuring the freshest of the garden's bounty.

Potato Salad with Bay Shrimp, Bacon & Arugula

This red, white and blue salad is perfect for a Fourth of July party. Peruvian potatoes are becoming more available at larger super markets. You may substitute Yukon gold or white rose potatoes.

Yield: 10-12 servings

1 pound Peruvian blue potatoes
1 pound red new potatoes
1 pound small white new potatoes
12 slices smoked bacon-fried crisp, chopped coarsely
4 hard boiled eggs, chopped
½ cup mayonnaise
1½ cups sour cream
1 lemon
1 cup green onions, finely chopped
Salt & pepper to taste
12 ounces bay shrimp
1 bunch arugula for garnish

With skins on, cook the three kinds of potatoes separately in rapidly boiling, lightly salted water. Do not overcook. Centers should still be slightly firm. Cool & quarter. Peel only the Peruvian potatoes. Place in large mixing bowl. Add the bacon, eggs, mayonnaise, and sour cream to the bowl. With a zester remove the zest from the lemon and add to the bowl. Cut the lemon in half and squeeze all the juice into the bowl through a small strainer to catch the seeds. Add the green onion, salt and pepper and toss gently.

Serve the salad on a platter, topped with the bay shrimp, and garnish generously with the arugula leaves, forming a wreath around the salad.

Chef Roy Harland

Harland's Sweet Potato Fries

Yield: 6-8 servings

10 sweet potatoes
Cornstarch to coat
Oil for deep frying
Salt to taste

Use sweet potatoes or yams. Peel and cut length-wise into about ¼-inch diameter pieces. Rinse, drain and, while still damp, toss in cornstarch. In a fry basket or strainer, shake off any excess cornstarch. Heat plenty of vegetable oil in a deep pan to 350°. Fry for about 3 minutes. Drain on paper towels, salt lightly and serve with jalapeño-arugula mayonnaise.

Jalapeño-Arugula Mayonnaise

1 whole egg
2 egg yolks
10 medium garlic cloves
2-5 fresh jalapeño peppers
2 cups vegetable oil
1 bunch arugula or watercress, coarsely chopped
1½ tablespoons Dijon mustard
1½ teaspoons fresh lemon juice
1½ teaspoons salt
½ teaspoon fresh ground pepper

In a food processor or blender, combine egg, egg yolks, garlic and jalapeños, blend well. While machine is running, drip oil into egg mixture until it emulsifies. Process until smooth and thick. Process arugula into sauce. Add mustard, lemon juice, salt and pepper.

Chef Roy Harland

Hosts: Robert Ancheta, The Ripe Tomato

Interior designer Robert Ancheta's list of clients includes such luminaries of the Hollywood scene as Burt Reynolds, Steve McQueen, James & Gloria Stewart, Ronald & Nancy Reagan …well, you get the idea. Guests enjoyed a tour of Robert's fascinating home and garden in Old Fig Garden before sitting down to the culinary talents of Chef Rudy Liebl. One of Fresno's famous balmy summer nights provided the perfect backdrop for this event.

Chicken Tarragon en Puff Pastry

Yield: 6 servings

Chicken Roll

6 half chicken breasts, boned
2 cups boiled fresh spinach
½ cup chopped pecans
2 cups sliced mushrooms
6 sheets puff pastry
3 cups heavy cream
1 teaspoon fresh tarragon
Salt & pepper, to taste

Remove skin from chicken breast, place between two sheets of plastic wrap and pound flat. Mix spinach and pecans, put on each chicken breast, then put mushrooms on top. Roll the breast jelly-roll style, from the side not the end. Salt and pepper the roll to taste.

Cut puff pastry sheet in half. Use rolling pin to thin sheet slightly, especially the edges. Place chicken roll on top of a sheet of puff pastry, trim ends to 1-inch from chicken, roll, dampen and seal edge and ends. Brush with egg wash (1 beaten egg with 1 teaspoon water). Bake at 350° for 30 minutes or until golden brown.

Place cream in sauce pan on top of stove; add tarragon, salt and pepper. Reduce until thickened. Divide sauce on serving plates. Slice chicken rolls, place on sauce. Serve immediately with rice and fresh al dente vegetables.

Chef Rudy Liebl, The Ripe Tomato

Host: Larry Balakian

This unique journey began at Fresno's Holy Trinity Armenian Church, the oldest Armenian church in America. Snacking along the way, sojourners next toured several more churches, ending at St. Paul Armenian Church. A seven-course Armenian dinner and mini-concert at St. Paul's Theatre followed, and as a final treat, coffee cup reader, Madame Hazel Arakalian, read each guest's fortune sending everyone home sated and satisfied.

Victoria's Shish Kebab

Yield: 6 servings

1 boned leg of lamb (1 pound per person)

Marinade

1 medium onion, minced
1 medium onion, sliced
½ cup chopped parsley
½ cup chopped fresh basil
1 tablespoon black pepper
1 tablespoon salt
3 tablespoons olive oil
1 clove crushed garlic
1 cup Burgundy wine
½ cup vinegar

Vegetables

3 green peppers, coarsely chopped
3 tomatoes, coarsely chopped
2 eggplants, cut into chunks
½ cup melted butter

Remove tissue and fat from meat, cut into 1½-inch cubes. Combine the 10 marinade ingredients in a glass container, then add meat. Marinate lamb for 24 hours. During the marinating time, toss the meat 5 or 6 times so the meat will be well coated. Thread meat on skewers and barbecue over wood from grape stumps. Let stumps burn down to coals before starting to cook. Turn skewers often so meat will cook evenly and brown on all sides. Do not overcook. Save marinade onions to add to cooked meat. Skewer vegetables, brush with butter and barbecue until just tender.

Victoria Balakian

Hosts: Julie O'Kane, Frank & Sally Smith, Dean & Nancy Blankinship, Chris & Claudine Mariscotti

This progressive dinner excursion was a rare opportunity to tour four luxurious homes built in the Barsotti area of Madera during the 1950's and 1960's. The city of Madera plays a vital part in the San Joaquin Valley's historical past. Guests enjoyed champagne, wine and gourmet food as guests, tales of the past and fine dining mingled, producing another special moment in history to be remembered.

Grilled Lamb Chops with Fresh Peach Chutney

This favorite family recipe is from Sunset Magazine, July 1986.

Yield: 4 servings

8-10 lamb chops
Salt & pepper to taste
¼ cup sugar
¼ cup cider vinegar
1 small onion, minced
½ cup Sun-Maid® raisins
1 teaspoon cinnamon
1 teaspoon ginger
3 medium ripe peaches, peeled, pitted, sliced ¼-inch thick.

Sprinkle chops with salt and pepper to taste; grill chops 3-4 minutes on each side. While chops cook, combine the following for chutney: sugar, vinegar, onions, raisins, cinnamon and ginger in frying pan. Stir frequently until onions are limp and raisins are plump, about 5 minutes. Add peaches and gently stir until they are hot, about 3 minutes. Spoon chutney on top of rib chops prior to serving.

Dean & Nancy Blankinship

Hosts: Jack & Margaret Thorburn, Steve & Sue Jacoby, Dawn Jacoby, Karen Humphrey, Ken Clarke, Dave & Linda Grubbs, Ron Rempel, Bill & Barbara Canning

The Blossom Trail is a Central Valley floral extravaganza put on by nature every spring. Party travelers board a deluxe bus for an hour-long tour of the beautiful blooms, ending with dinner along the Kings River. Hosts collaborate each year on a theme for the party; this year a Mexican theme prevailed with the hosts contributing a variety of regional dishes to enjoy with traditional margaritas. Olé!

Tamale Pie

This is mom's basic recipe. You may want to divide into 2 containers and freeze half for later.

Yield: 12-15 servings

1 pound ground round
1 large onion, chopped
1 clove garlic, chopped
½ cup oil
1 tablespoon salt
3 tablespoons chili powder
Dash cayenne pepper
1¾ cups canned diced tomatoes
2 cups cream-style corn
1 cup milk
1 cup yellow cornmeal
3 beaten eggs
1 cup ripe olives, whole, pitted

In a large pan like a Dutch oven, lightly brown meat, onions and garlic in oil. Add salt, chili powder, cayenne pepper, tomatoes and corn. Cook slowly for 15 minutes. Mix milk and cornmeal with eggs, add to first mixture, add olives. Pour into well oiled 9 x 12-inch pan and bake in 350° oven for 30 minutes.

Margaret Thorburn

Host: Cappie Barrett

Renowned hostess Cappie Barrett welcomed guests to her own private Tara, Barrett Manor, for a traditional plantation gala, complete with southern cooking, mint juleps, croquet on the lawn and banjo music. Mark Twain made an appearance to offer a few insights about his life, times and adventures as a world traveler. Rhett and Scarlett were there too, of course.

Sweet Southern Biscuits

Cake flour makes these biscuits lighter and fluffier, but 2 cups all-purpose flour can be used. Southern flour is superior to Yankee flour for light and fluffy baking. Sugar may be omitted for plain, but delicious biscuits. You can also dip a sugar cube in orange juice, place in center of each biscuit before baking. Substitute butter for shortening for a crisp biscuit.

Yield: 9 biscuits

1 cup self-rising flour
1 cup plus 2 tablespoons cake flour
1 tablespoon baking powder
1 tablespoon sugar
⅓ cup chilled vegetable shortening
⅔ cup buttermilk
2 large eggs, divided
¼ teaspoon water

Sift flours, baking powder and sugar into a large bowl. Cut in shortening until mixture resembles cornmeal. Make a well in the center of the flour mixture and pour in buttermilk and 1 egg. Blend until mixed. Turn dough onto a board, lightly floured with cake flour. Knead just until dough forms a ball. Add more cake flour as needed. Gently press out to ½-inch thickness. Cut with a floured 3-inch round biscuit cutter. Cut straight down-do not twist cutter. Place biscuits on ungreased baking sheet. Beat remaining egg and ¼ teaspoon water and brush on tops of biscuits. Bake at 350° for 15-20 minutes or until tops are golden brown. Serve hot or room temperature, with butter, honey, jam or jelly.

Cappie Barrett

Host: Rick Ataide, Vallis Restaurant

Kingsburg's popular mayor, Gordon Satterberg, hosted four visitors to his Swedish village. They dined at Kingsburg's renowned, Vallis Restaurant. Before dinner, the guests enjoyed a limousine tour around town with the mayor. It provided a wealth of conversation starters. James Vallis and Kathy Finnegan selected fine wines to accompany the savory French meal, served at a table Rick Ataide had artfully enhanced with candelabra and fresh flowers.

Bongo Bongo Soup

Yield: 6 servings (2½ quarts)

¾ pound spinach, fresh or frozen
1 8-ounce can of oysters, drained
2 quarts chicken stock
1 medium potato, peeled, grated
Salt to taste
¼ pound butter
¼ cup powdered milk

Simmer all ingredients, except butter and powdered milk, for about 20 minutes. Take off heat and allow to cool slightly. Blend the broth and the solids in the blender with a portion of the butter and powdered milk until all is used. Strain through cheesecloth, then taste. The soup may be adjusted with a little more salt, powdered milk, butter or potato, or a combination.

Vallis Restaurant

MENU

Paté De James and Assorted Hors d'oeuvres
Vallis' Champagne Cocktail

Bongo Bongo Soup
Morgan Sauvignon Blanc

Black Peppercorn Filet Mignon
Lockwood Reserve Cabernet Sauvignon

Peach Melba
Quady Essencia

Hosts: The City Press, Millerton State Park

Guests attired in their western duds were greeted to this old-fashioned hoedown by friendly folk handing out sarsaparilla. The patio of historic Millerton Courthouse on the shores of Millerton Lake was decorated with bales of hay, terra cotta potted plants and banners. After a lip-smacking barbecue, guests were confronted with a dazzling spread of blue-ribbon homemade ice creams and cobblers. When the sun went down, everyone enjoyed line dancing under the stars to lively country western tunes. A rib-tickling time was had by all!

Berry Cobbler

Fresh berries can be used–but this recipe calls for frozen. Use your favorite berries, such as raspberry, blackberry, boysenberry, or blueberry.

Yield: 8 to 10 servings

2 cups shifted all-purpose flour
¼ cup plus 4 tablespoons sugar
3 teaspoons baking powder
½ teaspoon salt
½ cup butter or margarine
¼ cup milk
2 eggs slightly beaten
2 packages of 16-ounce berries
¼ cup sugar (or more to taste)
1 tablespoons quick-cooking tapioca
1 tablespoons butter or margarine.

Topping: combine flour, 4 tablespoons sugar, baking powder and salt. Cut butter into flour mixture until it looks like coarse crumbs. Combine milk and eggs then add to dry mixture all at once; stir just to moisten. Set aside.

Filling: defrost frozen berries. Mix berries, ¼ cup sugar, tapioca together and let stand for five minutes. Put on low-medium heat and cook until slightly thickened and bubbly. Stir frequently to prevent sticking and burning. Stir in butter or margarine.

Pour hot filling into a 9 x 9-inch baking dish. Immediately spoon topping onto mixture in 6 to 8 equal amounts. Bake at 400˚ for about 20-25 minutes until golden brown.

Lynda Daley

Hosts: Don & Kathie McCollister, Bill & Anna Wattenbarger

Teams of four raced their way through the Fresno/Madera countryside searching for clues that led them ever forward past fascinating points of interest to their ultimate goal: barbecue dinner accompanied by Butterfield's award-winning beers (root beer too) at the McCollister residence along the cooling river. Decorations for the event were checkered flags and black and white checked pennants. Everyone ended up a winner!

Butterfield's Corn & Carrot Salad

This colorful salad is great for picnics or elegant parties. Sun-Maid® raisins can be added for more sweetness and color.

Yield: 4 cups

1 cup frozen corn, cooked slightly
3 cups (6 large) grated carrots
1 large clove chopped garlic
Salt & pepper to taste

Mix all ingredients together. Moisten with dressing below.

Raspberry Vinaigrette

Yield: about 1½ cups

½ cup raspberry vinegar
½ teaspoon Worcestershire sauce
⅓ teaspoon salt
⅓ teaspoon black pepper
¾ tablespoon sugar
1¼ tablespoon water
1 tablespoon beaten egg
1 cup salad oil

Blend all ingredients, except salad oil, in blender on #2 speed, then slowly add salad oil.

Butterfield's Brewing Company

Hosts: James & Coke Hallowell, Joyce Aiken

Winemaker Joel Aiken of Beaulieu Winery and Amy Aiken, consulting enologist, were on hand to offer a selection of premium wines during a five-course dinner in the Hallowell's extraordinary home in the foothills north of Friant. A change in the weather, however, resulted in an innovative solution to the outdoor dining plans. Artist friends converted the Hallowell's garage into a colorful Italian villa. White walls were hand-painted with murals and drapes were hung to conceal the garage doors. Doors leading to a storage room were artfully painted to depict wine cases and bottles, giving the impression of an abundant wine cellar. Friends can still enjoy this artfully decorated garage—after the party, the Hallowells left it in place!

Stuffed Roast Pork Loin

Yield: 8 servings

¼ cup salt
¼ cup sugar
2 quarts water
2 bay leaves
1 tablespoons allspice berries
1 tablespoons dried thyme
3 pounds pork tenderloin
2 cloves garlic, left whole
2 large shallots, finely chopped
3 tablespoons olive oil, divided
1 tablespoon water
½ pound country ham or prosciutto, finely chopped
2 tablespoons fresh rosemary leaves, finely chopped
1 cup unsalted chicken stock
2 tablespoons Dijon mustard
4 tablespoons unsalted butter

Mix salt, sugar, water, bay leaves, allspice and thyme in a pan and heat until the salt and sugar are dissolved. Let cool. Place meat in a small pan and pour the brine over the pork. Marinate for 6 hours in the refrigerator. Remove pork and wipe dry. With the handle of a wooden spoon, poke a hole carefully through the center of the tenderloin. Place garlic, shallots, 1 tablespoon of oil and 1 tablespoon water in a small sauté pan and heat for 10 minutes. Do not brown. Stir in ham and half the rosemary. Set aside to cool. When cool, push the mixture into the center of the loin. Mix the remaining oil and rosemary and rub over the meat. Let sit for 2 hours.

Heat oven to 325°. Heat a pan over high heat and sear loin, browning it on all sides. Put the loin in a roasting pan just large enough to hold it and cook for 30 minutes. Remove from oven and let sit for 20 minutes in a warm place covered with foil.

Remove any fat from pan, deglaze with stock; reduce to ½ cup, scraping the pan to dissolve browned meat juices. Strain stock into a saucepan. Whisk in the mustard and butter. Keep warm. Slice pork into ¼-inch slices. Put on hot plate and pour sauce over slices.

Joel and Amy Aiken

Leek & Sweet Potato Soup

Yield: 8 cups

2 tablespoons butter
2 leeks, wash well, slice (white part only)
1 medium onion, sliced
3 carrots, sliced
4 sweet potatoes or yams, peeled, quartered
Dash of thyme
1 bay leaf
⅓ cup chopped parsley
6 cups chicken stock
Salt & pepper
Dash of nutmeg
½ cup cream
Sliced chives
Buttered croutons

Melt butter in soup pot and sauté leeks and onions until translucent. Add carrots, potatoes, thyme, bay leaf and parsley. Cover with chicken stock. Bring to a boil, then simmer for 35 minutes. Season with salt, pepper, and nutmeg. Let cool. Puree 1-2 cups at a time in a blender or food processor. Stir in cream. Reheat before serving. Garnish with chives and croutons.

Joel and Amy Aiken

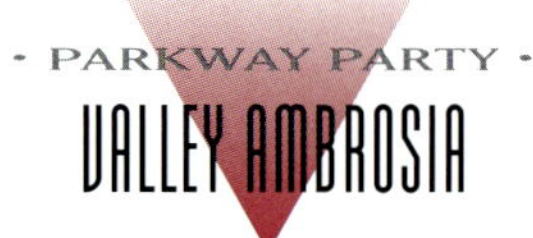

Hosts: James & Barbara Meinert

Horticulturist Pam Elam guided lucky participants through an unprecedented tour of the Kearney Ag Center, the University of California's state-of-the-art research facility. Guests sipped wine and sampled eight new and exotic varieties of peaches, nectarines and plums. A short jaunt took them to Kings River Community College for a guided tour of the school's ornamental horticultural gardens where dinner alfresco was served. Each guest took home a bag of luscious campus-grown fruit.

• PARKWAY PARTY •

SUNNYSIDE WILD WEST

Hosts: Steve & Lucille Pilibos

A team of massive Belgian horses pulled a festively-lit wagonload of guests on a tour of the Pilibos' Sunnyside ranch, while some of the guests chose to wander through the gardens on their own. Beer, wine, hors d'oeuvres and a barbecue extravaganza were available for the hungry travelers to feast upon. A square dance caller encouraged guests to try their hand (and feet) at some good old-fashioned square dancing. When the festivities drew to a close, guests were sent off with a gift of Lucille's hand-made apricot jam. No cowhand of the Old West ever had it so good!

Asparagus with Hollandaise

It never separates! This sauce takes about 5 minutes to prepare and it stays nice and thick. This recipe has been served at several Parkway functions and is always a great hit. Serve over fresh steamed vegetables, eggs Benedict, or your favorite fish.

Yield: 8 servings

7 egg yolks
2 dashes Tabasco sauce
1 tablespoon fresh lemon juice
¼ pound butter, melted
32-48 fresh asparagus spears

Place egg yolks, a splash of water and 2 shots of Tabasco in a double boiler, on very, very low heat. Stir constantly and continuously until mixture begins to thicken. Remove from heat, continue to stir while adding 2 teaspoons to 1 tablespoon fresh lemon juice, and enough melted butter, up to ¼ pound, to achieve desired consistency.

Select fresh asparagus, 4 to 6 per person. Trim ends and steam until al dente. Hollandaise sauce may be poured over center of asparagus, or served on the side.

Mike C. Brown, The Double Boilers

Lucille's Apricot Jam

Yield: 4½ pints

7 cups ripe fruit (cut cots in 6 or more slices)
1 package pectin
½ cup fresh lemon juice
7 cups sugar
½ teaspoon butter

In 8-quart sauce pan, mix fruit and pectin, add lemon juice. Bring fruit to slow boil, add sugar, stir constantly. Boil 4 minutes, add ½ teaspoon butter before 4 minutes is completed. Stir down, put in clean jars. Seal with hot paraffin wax to ⅛-inch from top.

Lucille Pilibos

Hosts: Edward & Terri Grootendorst, Roy Harland

The elegant house and gardens of this Gateway Bluffs estate provided the setting for an evening of nouvelle cuisine with unique accents. Chef Roy Harland displayed his special artistry with food in the kitchen, and at the table with his decorative presentation of each course. The palate was titillated with the textures and flavors; the eyes embraced the beauty; the nose inhaled the fragrance; this truly was an evening to savor.

MENU

FIRST COURSE

Sun-dried Pears with Roquefort and Pecans
Spicy Shrimp Toasts

SECOND COURSE

Lobster Timbales with Sauce Americaine
Mesclun Bouquet wrapped in Scottish Smoked Salmon with Champagne Vinaigrette
Kistler Dutton Ravel Chardonnay

THIRD COURSE

Wild Mushroom Risotto
Turned Carrots and Zucchini
Onion Straws
1987 Chalene Pinot Noir

FOURTH COURSE

Chocolate Cornucopia filled with White Chocolate Mousse and Raspberries
Quady Elysium
Coffee

Harland's Wild Mushroom Risotto

Yield: 8 cups

4 cups chicken stock, divided
1 ounce dried porcini mushrooms
8 ounces shiitake mushrooms
8 ounces cremini mushrooms
⅓ cup sweet butter, divided
1 diced yellow onion
½ cup dry white wine
2 cups rice
1 cup grated asiago cheese, divided
Salt & freshly ground black pepper to taste

In a small sauce pan, heat 1 cup of chicken stock to a simmer. Add porcini mushrooms, cover and remove from heat. Let stand 10 minutes, strain, reserving the infused stock. Chop porcinis coarsely. Wipe the fresh shiitake and cremini mushrooms with a damp towel and slice thinly. Heat half the butter in a sauté pan over medium heat. Sauté all mushrooms in the butter about 6 minutes, stirring occasionally, until well cooked and most of the liquid has evaporated, set aside. Heat remaining butter in a large sauté pan. Add onions and sauté over high heat a couple of minutes, add rice. Reduce heat to medium and cook the rice 2 to 3 minutes, stirring. Add the wine and cook until liquid mostly evaporated. Add the remaining stock, including the infused liquid, ½ cup at a time, stirring after each addition until the stock is absorbed. Continue in this fashion until all the stock has been added. After the final addition of stock, stir in the mushrooms, half the asiago and black pepper. The cheese is salty, but you may wish to add more salt. The risotto should be very moist and slightly firm to the bite. Garnish with additional asiago.

Chef Roy Harland

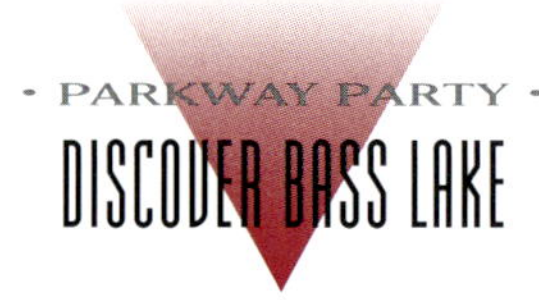

Host: The Pines Resort & Conference Center

Guests met on the front porch of Ducey's On The Lake before setting out for a first-time-ever tour of five of Bass Lakes' breathtakingly beautiful lakefront homes. Afterwards, a personalized welcome note and complimentary box of candy awaited guests in their chalet-like condos. At sunset, they were treated to a champagne cruise on the Bass Lake Queen, followed by an exceptionally fine dining experience at Ducey's. After an overnight stay and an elegant breakfast, the spoiled and pampered guests reluctantly left the next day, taking with them a warm glow of contentment.

MENU

FIRST COURSE

Belgian Onion Consommé
Savory Herb Biscotti

SECOND COURSE

Lobster and Chicken Quenelles
Cottonwood Canyon 1990 Barrel Select Chardonnay

THIRD COURSE

Fresh Baby Greens
Roasted Hazelnuts
Balsamic Blackberry Vinaigrette
Trio of Melon Sorbet

FOURTH COURSE

Roulades of Beef
Mushroom Duxelles
Petite Halibut en Papillote
Chipotle Cream Sauce
Rosemary and Garlic Crusted Potatoes
Langtry 1989 Meritage of Red

FIFTH COURSE

Gran Marnier Soufflé
Bitter Chocolate Sauce
Fine Reserve

Halibut en Papillote with Julienned Vegetables

Yield: 6 servings

2 pounds halibut fillet
1 medium carrot, cut into fine julienne
1 white leek, julienned, remove rootlet & leaf end
½ red pepper, cut into fine julienne
5 tablespoons butter, divided
6 tablespoons white wine
18 fresh tarragon leaves
1 egg white

Cut the halibut on a bias into 6 equal pieces. Gently sweat the carrots, leeks and red pepper in 2 tablespoons of butter until they soften, but do not brown.

Cut 6 sheets of parchment paper, 18 x 18-inches. Arrange each halibut piece slightly to the right of center on each sheet. Spoon the julienned vegetables over each piece of fish. Place ½ tablespoon butter atop each. Place 3 tarragon leaves on top of butter on each serving. Sprinkle each with wine.

Lightly beat egg white so that it breaks up; do not cause to foam. Brush the outer edges of parchment with egg white; seal by making a series of straight folds all along the edge of paper. Brush the folds with egg white and make another set of folds. The finished papillotes should form half circles. Bake papillotes on a sheet pan in a 350° oven until they puff, approximately 8-10 minutes.

The papillotes are best cut open in the dining room with scissors and transferred to hot plates in front of the diner. The natural juices in the bottom of the parchment sack are spooned over, or you may choose to serve in the parchment sack directly on the plate.

Chef David Pol

Hosts: Quady Winery, Silver Fox Winery, Rick Ataide, Steven Croff, Gorgeous Foods

The mood was casual, the setting sublime, the food was gorgeous, the wine divine. Guests spent an evening under the stars, strolling the grounds of Quady Winery with the vintners of two outstanding local wineries who answered their questions and shared samplings of their latest releases. Gorgeous Foods provided a delectable supper, impeccably prepared. A perfect way to end the day!

Gelsamina's Chocolate Pudding Cake

Mom, Gelsamina, adds a couple of extra ingredients to a quality box mix and produces a fabulous cake. All will believe you made this luscious cake from scratch!

Yield: 8-10 servings

The Cake

1 box Swiss Chocolate Cake mix
1 teaspoon baking soda
1 cup buttermilk
3 eggs

Preheat oven to 350°. Grease and dust two 9-inch round cake pans; line with wax or parchment paper.

Mix the cake ingredients, following the directions on the box exactly. Combine rest of ingredients then add to cake mixture. Use the spatula to spread the cake mixture evenly in the cake pans. Bake at 350° for 35 minutes. Test for doneness with a toothpick inserted into middle of the cake. If no batter adheres, cake is done.

The Pudding Filling

Select a large box of chocolate instant pudding, follow box directions for mixing, chill and allow to set.

The Frosting

3 tablespoons butter
3 squares unsweetened chocolate
1 teaspoon vanilla
⅓ cup milk
1 large egg
2 cups sifted powdered sugar

In a double boiler, melt the butter and chocolate. Set the pan over ice. Add the vanilla, milk, egg and powdered sugar. Beat ingredients with a hand mixer on high speed to a frosting thickness and texture. Do not over-beat.

Insert skewers crosswise into the middle of each cake. Insert a serrated knife into the side center of the cake. Rotating the cake clockwise, cut around and into the center of the cake, making a total of 4 layers. Note: In order to keep the cake level when stacking, reverse the cake so that the top and bottom layer face each other. Frost the outside of the layers. Spread the pudding on three layers, then stack layers. The top layer will be frosted with the frosting.

Frost the cake on the top and sides, making swirl designs. Garnish with chopped nuts, shaved chocolate or fresh sliced strawberries. Serve the cake and say 'I Love You' with chocolate!

Chef Nancy Vajretti

Hosts: California State Parks & Recreation-San Joaquin District, Friends of Millerton

Over twenty souls braved the cold morning temperature and gathered at Millerton Lake for a unique opportunity to observe our national emblem, the American Bald Eagle, in its winter habitat. To begin, a slide show of eagles around the world was shown at the Millerton Courthouse. Before the Eagle's Eye barge cast off, Captain Jim cautioned participants that all marriages performed while underway were valid only for the duration of the trip. During the three-hour excursion, three bald eagles, one golden eagle, one osprey, and an assortment of hawks and water fowl appeared for this special engagement.

Fire Brigade Chili

If you want to take a walk on the wild side, substitute venison or elk for the beef. Preparation time is 35 minutes, cooking time 1½ to 2 hours.

Yield: 6 cups

3 pounds beef chuck, diced
3 cups water
1 cup beef broth
1 8-ounce can tomato sauce
6 tablespoons garlic powder
¼ cup hot chili powder
¼ cup mild chili powder
3 tablespoons cumin
3 tablespoons minced onion
2 tablespoons paprika
1 tablespoon ground pepper (don't stub your toe when measuring this)
1 tablespoon sugar
2 teaspoons salt
Suggested garnishes: chopped tomato, green onion, shredded cheddar cheese, sour cream.

Brown meat in a large skillet over high heat, in three batches, transferring to a Dutch oven with a slotted spoon. Add remaining ingredients to Dutch oven. Bring to boil; reduce heat and simmer uncovered, stirring occasionally, 1½ to 2 hours. Garnish as desired.

Hardin Weaver

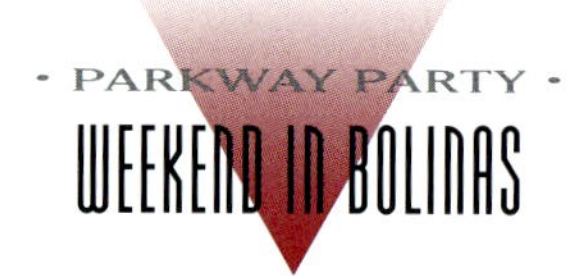

Hosts: Jack & Margaret Thorburn

For a fantastic coastal retreat, guests enjoyed a cottage in Bolinas overlooking the Pacific Ocean. They spent a weekend viewing San Francisco from a hot tub, discovering Audubon Canyon Ranch and the egret and heron rookeries, walking the earthquake trail, visiting artist Keith Hansen's studio, surfing at the Bolinas/Stinson lagoon inlet and hiking Mt. Tamalpais. From Friday afternoon to Sunday evening, it was an unforgettable treat.

Swedish Pancakes

These are also called Dutch Boy Pancakes. This is a great recipe! It's traditional for Bolinas weekends and is always a favorite. Our daughter was an exchange student in Sweden and lived in the Governor's Palace. The recipe was a favorite of the Governor's wife.

Yield: 4 servings

4 eggs
1 cup milk
½ cup flour
¼ teaspoon salt
1 tablespoon butter
Suggested condiments: yogurt, sour cream, jam, fresh fruit, maple syrup

Beat eggs, add milk and beat more. Combine flour and salt. Blend alternately with egg mixture. Can be beaten by hand or blender. Melt butter in deep heavy pan, a 10-inch cast iron skillet or equivalent glass baking dish. Place mixture in pan and bake immediately in 325° oven, until slightly brown and puffed, about 20-25 minutes. Cut into wedges. Serve with sour cream, jam and fresh fruit, or syrup.

Serve the champagne and coffee while pancake is cooking. Serve the pancake quickly with a flourish, while it is still puffed. Bake more pancakes as guests are enjoying the first.

Margaret Thorburn

Hosts: John & Brooke Wissler, Teresa Hurtado

The ancients knew the importance of this date, the point at which the sun swings outward to the farthest reaches of its ecliptic—before swinging back once more to reaffirm that all's still right in our universe. The sheltering elms of the Mordecai ranch, along Cottonwood Creek in Madera County, was the setting for a delectable dinner furnished by caterer Teresa Hurtado. The spirit of the Druids presided over all for an evening of enchantment.

Apple & Teriyaki Grilled Salmon

Serve salmon with new potato flowers and grilled vegetables.

Yield: 6 servings

Marinade

¾ cup apple cider
6 tablespoons soy sauce
2 tablespoons unsalted butter
1 large garlic clove, peeled
1 apple, sliced
6 fresh salmon steaks or filets

Mix apple cider, soy sauce, butter and garlic clove in a sauce pan, bring to boil. Turn off heat and set until cool. Add apple slices. Marinate fresh salmon overnight in refrigerator.

Grill: Arrange salmon steaks on a grill about 6 inches above a bed of hot coals. Cook, turning once, until just opaque but still moist, about 10 minutes.

Broil: Arrange salmon filets, skin side up, on a greased rack in a 12 x 15-inch broiler pan. Broil 3 to 4 inches below heat, turning once and brushing with remaining marinade, until fish is just opaque but still moist in thickest part, about 6 to 8 minutes.

Teresa Hurtado Catering

New Potato Flowers

Yield: 6 servings

12 2 to 3-inch red potatoes, skins on
¼ cup clarified butter
¼ cup sour cream
¼ cup chives, chopped fine
Salt & pepper (optional)

Wash potatoes well, then dry and roast until just tender. Sauté in clarified butter for 5 minutes. Make two cuts to about 1-inch from bottom of potato. Squeeze potato slightly to open petals. Put 1 teaspoon of sour cream in center, sprinkle with chives. Salt and pepper to taste. To clarify butter: melt butter; skim foam off top; carefully pour off clear (clarified) butter, leaving milk fat residue in bottom of pan.

Chef Teresa Hurtado

Hosts: Roger Rocka & Jan Mitchell, Weldon Schapansky, Bob & Joanne Lippert, Clem & Dorothy Renzi

Why Wilson? What a question! Because Wilson Avenue happens to be one of the real treasures of residential Fresno. Partygoers enjoyed a memorable evening touring four historic homes and gardens in the Old Fig Garden area. A stroll down Wilson began with cocktails and hors d'oeuvres at the first home, then on to the next for salad. At the third stop, the main course was prepared by Seen Lippert, chef at Berkeley's Chez Panisse. The trip concluded with dessert and a bonus: a mini rock and roll operetta performed by Dorothy Renzi. Great food, great setting, great company. No need to ask, why Wilson?

Ratatouille

We served this with roasted pork and natural pan juices. You can hardly miss with these great summer vegetables, served warm or cold, ratatouille is delicious!

Yield: 8-9 cups

1½ pound eggplant skin on, cut into ¼-inch cubes
Salt & pepper
½ cup pure olive oil, divided
2 tablespoons water
2 medium yellow onions, sliced
4 red or yellow bell peppers, cut ¼-inch slices
4 zucchini, green or yellow, cut into ¼-inch slices
1 pound tomatoes (3-4) peeled, seeded, diced
2 cloves garlic, minced
4 tablespoons mixed fresh herbs: basil, thyme, parsley, chopped
2 tablespoons balsamic vinegar
1 tablespoon red wine vinegar
2 teaspoons capers
Extra virgin olive oil

Toss eggplant with salt and pepper, 2 tablespoons of olive oil and water. Place in a baking dish, cover and bake at 375° for 45 minutes, or until tender. Drain any excess liquid.

Sauté onions in 2 tablespoons olive oil until softened and lightly browned, remove and set aside. In the same pan, sauté the peppers with 1 tablespoon olive oil until tender. Season with salt and pepper, set aside with onions. Sauté the squash in remaining oil until softened. Season with salt and pepper.

Place all vegetables, including eggplant, back into the pan. Add tomatoes and garlic and cook for 15 minutes. If the mixture is too runny, pour off the excess juices and reduce them until thickened. Add reduced juices back to vegetables, along with the herbs, capers and vinegars. Simmer 10 minutes more. Correct seasoning and splash with extra virgin olive oil. Serve warm or cool to room temperature.

Chef Seen Lippert

Hosts: Erna Kubin-Clanin, Franko Cardoza, Rick Ataide, Steve Croff
Back to the Future Reunion Limousines

Picture a terrace on a sublime midsummer night, a table of shimmering china, glowing crystal, and lovingly arranged bouquets. Hear the sweet sounds of classical guitar and harp melodies playing in the night air. The towering pines surrounding you, and the majestic shadow of Chateau du Sureau is behind you. From the Elderberry House kitchen aromas of freshly roasted game, sweet succulent vegetables, divine desserts and vintage wines tantalize the senses. Transportation by luxurious limousine adds additional refinement to this grand gastronomical event.

MENU CARTE SUREAU

Champagne and Elderberry Nectar

FIRST COURSE
Sea Scallops in Pear Puff
Assorted Grilled Squash
Merryvale Sauvignon Blanc

SECOND COURSE
Artichoke Soup with Tarragon
Artichoke "Chips"
Merryvale Starmont Chardonnay

THIRD COURSE
Iced Terrine of Ruby Grapefruit
with Banana Coulis

FOURTH COURSE
Grilled "Duck Steak"
Persimmon-Mustard Sauce
Potato Noodles
Sautéed Spinach, Watercress and Sweet Corn
Caramelized Pearl Onions with Asparagus
Gary Farrell 1992 Bien Nacido Pinot Noir

FIFTH COURSE
Arugula Salad with Orange Sections and Beets
Citrus Vinaigrette

SIXTH COURSE
Crepaze of Hazelnut and White Chocolate Mousse
with Raspberry Sauce and Warm Apple Tart with
Caramel Royal and Vanilla Ice Cream
Quady Elysium

Artichoke Soup with Tarragon & Artichoke Chips

Yield: 8-10 servings

3 large artichokes, set aside one for chips
1 medium potato, peeled, quartered
2 tablespoons chopped fresh tarragon, divided
8 cups chicken stock
½ cup sour cream
2 tablespoons sherry
Salt & pepper
Cooking oil for deep frying chips

Remove all leaves, stem and choke from artichokes, reserving bottoms only. Poach in water for about one hour, until soft but still slightly firm. Remove with slotted spoon and add 2 artichoke bottoms, potato and 1 tablespoon of tarragon to large saucepan with chicken stock. Simmer for 30 minutes, puree in blender and return to pan. Whisk in sour cream and sherry, salt and pepper. Reheat and serve immediately. Garnish with remaining tarragon.

Artichoke Chips

On a diagonal, thinly slice the reserved cooked artichoke bottom into chips. Heat oil to 350°. Submerge artichoke chips into oil with a sieve for 2 minutes or until crisp. Remove and let dry over kitchen towel.

Erna's Elderberry House Kitchen

Hosts: Crystal Falls Inn, Radanovich Winery, Limo For You, Back to the Future Reunion, An Elegant Affair Limousines

Partygoers traveled by limo to Crystal Falls Inn, nestled alongside a beautiful stretch of Lewis Creek where it flows through the Oakhurst/Bass Lake area of the Sierras. Each windowed table of the Inn offers a view of the coursing water and the ducks, squirrels and other wildlife that abound in the area. Diners were greeted with a wine-tasting opportunity on the deck, followed by a dinner that equaled the delightful atmosphere.

Stuffed Breast of Chicken with Asiago Cheese Sauce & Pine Nuts

Yield: 4 servings

4 cloves garlic, minced, divided
5 tablespoons butter, divided
5 tablespoons extra virgin olive oil, divided
1 cup fresh mushrooms, roughly chopped
2 cups fresh spinach, roughly chopped
2 tablespoons fresh bread crumbs
4 10-ounce boneless chicken breasts
2 tablespoons flour
2 cups milk
1 cup asiago cheese, grated
½ cup champagne
2 tablespoons fresh parsley, finely chopped
4 tablespoons roasted pine nuts
Salt to taste

Stuffing

Sauté garlic in 2 tablespoons each butter and olive oil, add mushrooms, spinach and bread crumbs, combine and set aside.

Chicken Rolls

Pound chicken filets to ⅛-inch thickness, between 2 sheets of plastic wrap. Lay chicken breasts flat, fill with approximately 2 tablespoons of stuffing; roll jelly roll fashion, from wide side. Brown breasts in 1 tablespoon each olive oil and butter, using tongs to turn. Place in oven-proof pan; bake at 400° for 20 minutes.

Asiago Cheese Sauce

Sauté 2 cloves minced garlic in 2 tablespoons each butter and olive oil, add flour and cook for 2 minutes. Add milk and cook, stirring constantly until mixture comes to a boil. Reduce heat; add asiago cheese; cook for 1 minute, add champagne, simmer 5 minutes. Take sauce off heat and stir in parsley. Set aside, keep warm.

Slice chicken rolls diagonally and serve with asiago cheese sauce. Sprinkle with roasted pine nuts.

Crystal Falls Inn

Hosts: Bill Minschew, Rick Ataide, The Daily Planet

Known worldwide for his bamboo inspired works of art, Bill Minschew lives and works in one of the most unusual homes in the Valley. At his hilltop abode, guests enjoyed a summer night's northwest breeze as it caressed and slowly wafted away the day's solar heating. As moonlight displaced a fading sunset, conversations turned cosmic. Out-of-this-world cuisine further enhanced a truly intergalactic evening. Lovers, stargazers, gourmets and connoisseurs alike were enthralled with this star-studded evening.

Chocolate Tacos with White Chocolate Mousse

Praline Taco Shells

Yield: 4-6 tacos

¼ cup butter or margarine
¼ cup firmly packed brown sugar
¼ cup light corn syrup
3½ tablespoons all-purpose flour
½ cup finely chopped pecans, walnuts or almonds
1 teaspoon vanilla

Melt butter in a pan over low heat. Add sugar and corn syrup. Bring to a boil over high heat, stirring constantly; remove from heat and stir in flour and nuts until blended. Stir in vanilla.

Line baking sheet with parchment paper (it must be flat, not warped). Place 2 to 3 tablespoons of the batter on baking sheet, position cookies 8 inches apart, and at least 4 inches from side of sheet. If batter does not flow easily, evenly press or spread it out to a 3 to 4-inch circle. Bake in a 325° oven until a rich golden brown all over, about 12 minutes. Cool on the baking sheet, on a rack, until slightly firm, about 1 minute. When cookie edges are just firm enough to lift, loosen edges with a spatula. Lift cookie (it should still be flexible, but firm enough to move without pulling apart). Drape cookie over a rounded edge to form taco. If taco becomes too firm to shape, return to oven for a few minutes, until pliable. Let shaped taco cool until firm, about 2 minutes. Gently remove from mold.

Chocolate Glaze

Melt 1 pound of semisweet chocolate in double boiler or microwave. Use a deep bowl to hold chocolate glaze, allowing plenty of room to coat taco. Dip tacos vertically into melted glaze to coat ½ of taco. Reserve some of the glaze for decorating dessert plate. If not serving immediately, place tacos side by side (not touching) on parchment lined baking sheet. Store in freezer until ready to fill.

White Chocolate Mousse

Yield: 10-12 servings

6½ ounces white chocolate
1½ teaspoon unflavored gelatin
¾ cup cold water
4 egg yolks
¼ cup sugar
4 egg whites
½ cup sugar
2 cups whipping cream
1½ to 2 cups fruit, cut into bite-size pieces

Melt white chocolate over double boiler or in microwave. Soak gelatin in cold water for 5 minutes, until soft. Whip egg yolks with ¼ cup sugar until ribbon stage, set aside. Over double boiler, bring egg whites and ½ cup sugar to 107° F (or until warm to lower lip), then whip until stiff peaks form. Set aside. Whip cream until stiff, set aside. Heat gelatin over gentle heat until dissolved and liquified, then mix into melted chocolate. Fold egg yolks into chocolate mixture; fold in the meringue; fold in the whipped cream. Chill for 2 to 3 hours. Fill Chocolate dipped praline taco shells just prior to serving. Garnish with fruit. Important to keep mousse chilled.

The Daily Planet

Hosts: Barry Kriebel, Gary Marshburn

Guests boarded the Raisin Express for a trip to the world's largest agricultural enterprise, the Sun-Maid Raisin Plant in Kingsburg. There were no dancing raisins in sight, but the president of Sun-Maid along with other officers led a special tour of the plant and gave details of the origin and history of this eighty-one-year-old Valley institution. After dining on the beautifully landscaped headquarters patio, guests were presented with a souvenir of their visit—raisins, of course.

Raisin Brown Bread

This is a V.I.P. recipe. Recipe can be halved to make one loaf, but you will want two. It's great!

Yield: 2 loaves

2 cups Sun-Maid® raisins, dark or golden
½ cup packed brown sugar
¼ cup butter
1 cup cornmeal
½ cup molasses
1 egg
2 cups buttermilk
2 cups whole-wheat flour
1 cup white flour
2 teaspoons baking soda

Preheat oven to 350°. Liberally coat the bottoms of two 8 x 4-inch loaf pans with margarine, dust with flour. Put raisins in bowl, cover with boiling water; let stand 5 minutes, drain. Cream sugar and butter. Add cornmeal, molasses, egg and buttermilk. Stir in wheat flour, white flour and baking soda. Add raisins. Pour into pans and bake for 40-50 minutes.

Pam Kriebel

Fruit Stuffed Pork Roast

Yield: 6 servings

3 pounds pork loin roast
1½ cup Sun-Maid® raisins (golden)
1 cup chopped pitted prunes
1 cup chopped tart apples
2 tablespoons dry bread crumbs
2 teaspoons fresh rosemary
½ teaspoon salt
½ cup apple brandy
½ cup apple cider

Preheat oven to 350°. Starting at narrow side of pork roast, cut a slit like a book. Mix raisins, prunes, apples, bread crumbs, rosemary and salt together; stuff pork; close and tie string around roast to secure. Place roast in pan. Mix brandy and cider together, use ¼ cup to baste roast; repeat basting frequently, adding a little more of mixture each time. Bake 1½ hours. Heat thermometer should register 160°. Serve with brandy sauce.

Pam Kriebel

Brandy Sauce

1 cup apple cider
½ cup brandy
2 teaspoons corn starch

Heat to boil. Continue cooking until thickens. Pour over roast.

Pam Kriebel

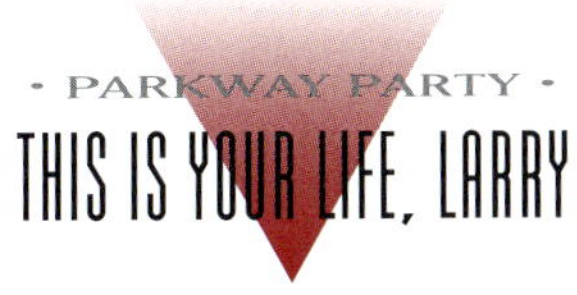

Hosts: Mary LaFollette, Anita Shanahan,
Coke Hallowell, Stacey Batrich-Smith

Heeere's Larry! Friends of Larry Balakian gathered at the Fresno Art Museum, scene of so many of Larry's "crimes", for fun, food and fashion, not to mention a few surprises. One of Fresno's acclaimed party-givers, it seemed appropriate to honor Larry with a party just for him. Larry, until then, had been unaware his mother had saved clothes from important events in his life. Imagine his surprise when familiar polyesters, paisleys, bell bottoms and Nehru jackets, along with ties from skinny to fat, were modeled for the assemblage by female friends of Larry. Accompanying this hilarious fashion show was a very special rendition of My Funny Valentine. A halt was called to the proceedings when a number of women were forced to retire to the ladies room to repair makeup ruined by the tears shed from happy laughter.

Larry's Salad

Larry Balakian conceived the idea for Parties for the Parkway and is co-chair of the committee. His salad is very popular at Parkway Parties—many have asked for the recipe.

Yield: Based on number of guests

The Salad

Take all the fresh vegetables and fruit ingredients you can find in your refrigerator that haven't wilted or grown mold. If in doubt, don't use! Cut all into bite-sized pieces, chill.

The Dressing

Gather various flavored vinegars, salad oils and spices, remove caps. Get out the largest bowl you own; close your eyes; pick up various bottles and pour or shake over the empty bowl. Open eyes. Wipe up any ingredients that missed the bowl. Mix the ingredients, taste test; adjust seasoning as needed. Pour salad ingredients into bowl and toss to coat, refrigerate until used. Often served in take out containers, but may be served in individual salad bowls or plates. Go into the yard; find the bush with the largest non-toxic leaves; wash and place one or two leaves on each serving plate; top with salad.

Larry Balakian (submitted without his knowledge)

MADELINE DAVIDSON'S RECIPES

· THE PARKWAY REMEMBERS ·

MADELINE DAVIDSON'S RECIPES

No book dedicated to Madeline would be complete without some of her recipes. Her family graciously gave permission to reprint some of the family favorites. We know—in addition to savoring the recipes—you will enjoy reading them, written in Madeline's delightful style. Some of the recipes come from Orange Kitchen Cookbook, written by Madeline.

Pears au Chocolate

Nancy Barg and I didn't have the nerve to make this separately the first time—so we got together for the peeling, poaching & dipping. We guarantee one of you can do it all alone—but if you feel you need moral support, call us:

Cook in large kettle for 15 minutes: **1 cup sugar, 4 cups water, the juice of 1 lemon, 2 cinnamon sticks + 4 cloves.** Add **8 peeled whole pears**, stems left on, and the bottoms cut flat to keep each pear standing, & poach for 30-40 minutes. Test with a toothpick. When tender, remove & chill pears overnight. The next day, dry the fruit with a paper towel & dip into the following batter: Heat over low heat **4 ounces unsweetened chocolate, 2 ounces semi-sweet chocolate, ½ cup sweet butter, softened.** Dip carefully; don't lose a stem. Let chocolate covered pears rest on a cake rack. Chill. Serve with candied violets & mint leaves atop. Gorgeous!

Peach Souffle

So much hot air, but it looks swell. Serve the coffee, and whip this up while the guests are still thinking crab casserole. Add: **1 cup sugar, pinch salt, 3 tablespoons orange juice** (one friend suggested Grand Marnier instead. Sometimes I use brandy bottled in our Valley) to: **1 jar Gerber's junior peaches.**

Beat **3 egg whites** stiff & fold in peach mix. Pour gently into buttered 1 quart casserole. Set in pan of hot water. Bake 375° 20 minutes. Serves 4. I've never had nerve enough to double the recipe – I always make 2 batches. "Chicken Cook!"

The Salmon Mousse

The Fig Garden area is the home of Ms. Renzi, musician; Ms. Erbes, artist; Mr. Levine, poet; Mr. Eaton, businessman; Mr. Shepard, lawyer & so forth. If I ever make the list of outstanding & talented Fig Garden residents, it will be on the strength of my salmon mousse recipe.

Mix **1 envelope (plus ¼ teaspoon) of Knox gelatin, 1 tablespoon sugar, ½ teaspoon salt & 1 teaspoon dry mustard** in a saucepan. Add **¼ cup water & ¼ cup white wine vinegar.** Dissolve over low heat. Off heat fold in **1 large can salmon**, drained & flaked, **½ cup each minced green onion & celery, 1 tablespoon capers, & ½ cup heavy cream, whipped.** Refrigerate in fish-shaped 3-cup mold. Or quadruple the recipe & borrow my economy sized Portuguese tin salmon mold—the *piece de resistance* at innumerable F. G. dinners, receptions, Bar Mitzvahs & book club lunches.

My Favorite Dessert or Plain Ole Jelly Roll

Beat **4 egg yolks** & add **¾ cup sugar**, & beat til creamy. Add **1 teaspoon vanilla**. Sift before measuring **¾ cup cake flour**. Resift with **¾ teaspoon baking powder**. Gradually add flour mix to egg-sugar & stir til smooth. Whip **4 eggs whites** til stiff with **¼ teaspoon salt** & fold them with a light hand into the cake batter. Line a 15 x 10-inch cookie sheet with an edge with heavy, greased, unglazed brown paper. Spread the dough in carefully & bake at 375° for 13 minutes. Turn the hot cake out on a towel sprinkled with powdered sugar. Peel the brown paper off—easy does it! Spread with a favorite jelly & roll. How lovely & light & old-fashioned.

First, off to Michael's to see if they have 1 dozen paper bibs emblazoned with big red lobsters (cows or chicken won't do). Buy them. Then you may have a:

Cioppino Party for 12

Buy 2½ **pounds sea bass** (ask for some of the bass fish trimmings) **2 crabs, 3 pounds shrimp, 3 dozen clams.** Cut the fish into good sized serving pieces. Clean & crack the crab (leaving it in the shells); save the top shell for making stock. Remove shrimp shells (not the tails) & devein (ugh!).

Make a fish fumet (I looked that up in my big all-purpose cookbook) with bass trimmings, crab shells & shrimp shells, and about **4½ cups water.** Simmer 20 minutes. You should have 3-4 cups of stock.

Saucetime: *(find the biggest pot in town or borrow mine)*
Sauté **2 sweet Italian sausages**, rough chopped, **2 onions** chopped, **2 green peppers**, chopped, in **¾ cups olive oil.** Add: **8 cloves of garlic, salt & pepper to taste, 2 large cans of tomatoes, 3 cups dry red table wine** (I use Gallo Paisano) **3 cups tomato juice, 2½ cups fish stock, 3 bay leaves, ¼ cup small handfuls or more (to taste) of parsley, 1 teaspoon basil & 1 teaspoon oregano.** Cook for 10 minutes. Add the **fish, cracked crab & shrimp**. Simmer for 5 minutes. Three! minutes before serving add the clams (in shells), cover & simmer until **clams** open.

Serve sprinkled with more fresh parsley to bibbed guests accompanied by soup spoons, cocktail forks, pliers and a hammer or two.

Cream of Lovely Lettuce

Cook ⅓ **cup minced green onion** in **3 tablespoons butter** for 5-10 minutes in a 2-quart pot. Do not brown. Stir in **4 packed cups of romaine lettuce strips & ½ teaspoon salt.** Cover & cook 5 minutes. Sprinkle with **3 tablespoons flour**. Cook 3 minutes, stirring. Add **5½ cups chicken broth or vegetable stock.** Cook again for 5 minutes. Puree in food mill (or blender if you're out of food mills this week). Set aside. Combine **2 egg yolks & ½ cup whipping cream.** Add slowly to soup & stir over low heat for a minute or two. Off heat add **1 tablespoon butter.** Serve to 6 lucky guests.

This is a reasonable facsimile of a fine soup served at a favorite southern Fresno County restaurant—I'm second-guessing them!

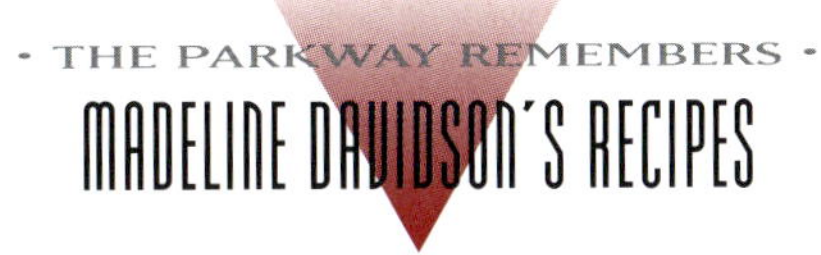

Gazpacho–or what to serve, beside gin & tonic, when the Thursday Afternoon Debauchery Society (TADS) comes to lunch on a 110° July afternoon.

(Back to the old chopping block)

Smash in a mortar or on HI in a blender

2 fat garlic cloves, 1 large onion,

3 tablespoons fresh parsley with 1½ teaspoon salt

Very finely chop:

3 large tomatoes, peeled

1 cucumber, seeded & peeled

1 green pepper

Mash with potato masher:

The two vegetable mixes, **¼ cup olive oil, 3 tablespoons wine vinegar, 1 teaspoon oregano**. Refrigerate til icy. Divide in soup bowls, add **1 ice cube** & top with a few **bread crumbs.**

Reprinted from Orange Kitchen Cookbook

If the south ever rises again, it might very well be on the strength of the

Hotel Roanoke's Spoon Bread

We Lynchburg ladies often drove down the Blue Ridge on a spring Sunday to this hospitable hostelry where one expected to be seated next to Clark Gable or Leslie Howard (in costume). Spoonbread came like clockwork with every entree on the menu.

Beat **5 eggs** with **2 cups milk**

Mix **1½ cups yellow cornmeal, 1 tablespoon baking powder, 1 teaspoon salt, 1 teaspoon sugar**. Scald with **1½ cups boiling water** (keep stirring). Add **½ cup cubed melted butter**. Add egg & milk mix.

Pour into a buttered flat table ready pan; bake 350° 30-40 minutes. Serve in place of starch or rolls.

Reprinted from Orange Kitchen Cookbook

Randolph Macon Women's College Shrimp Paste

Served to us girls behind the red brick wall in Main Hall Lobby at Sunday tea time. Our dates thought it was great (the shrimp stuff). Subsequently—I've discovered, husbands do, too.

Blend with electric mixer:

8 ounces cream cheese

Juice of ½ lemon

½ onion (grated over waxed paper-save juice)

½ teaspoon salt

Tabasco to taste

½ cup thick catsup (Heinz is good)

Add:

1 can cocktail shrimp, drained & coarsely chopped. If this seems too stiff, dribble in some onion juice.

Reprinted from Orange Kitchen Cookbook

HORS D'OEUVRES

SOUPS

SALADS

PASTA, RICE, AND OTHER SIDE DISHES

SALAD DRESSINGS & SAUCES

BREADS

BEVERAGES

VEGETABLES

ENTREES

DESSERTS

MADELINE DAVIDSON'S RECIPES